YOU'RE HIRED

THE ESSENTIAL GUIDE TO JOB HUNTING AND PERSONAL BRANDING

Tom O'Neil

NEW HOLLAND

First published in 2015 by New Holland Publishers Pty Ltd
London • Sydney • Auckland

The Chandlery Unit 9, 50 Westminster Bridge Road, London SE1 7QY, United Kingdom
1/66 Gibbes Street, Chatswood, NSW 2067, Australia
5/39 Woodside Ave, Northcote, Auckland 0627, New Zealand

www.newhollandpublishers.com

A record of this book is held at the British Library and the National Library of Australia.

ISBN: 978 1 74257 789 0

Managing Director: Fiona Schultz
Publisher: Christine Thomson
Editor: Anna Brett
Design: Thomas Casey
Production Director: Olga Dementiev
Printer: Toppan Leefung Printing Limited

10 9 8 7 6 5 4 3 2 1

Keep up with New Holland Publishers on Facebook
www.facebook.com/NewHollandPublishers

CONTENTS

INTRODUCTION

In the business of recruitment and human resources, I continually come into contact with candidates who have a good deal of potential. However, they are unable to demonstrate to me how they have added measurable value in their positions with previous and current employers, thereby failing to convince both myself and others to interview or recruit them.

The problem is that most people don't understand they are a 'brand' and have no idea how to actually 'sell' themselves effectively to potential employers. They don't realize that in the job hunt they become a product, which must highlight, in a tangible fashion, their best features and achievements in a way that ensures potential purchasers (résumé screeners and interviewers) will take notice.

The aim of this book is to help you understand the ways to increase your chances of gaining a dream job, through more effective selling of yourself with your résumé, during interviews and through networking.

When you sell yourself professionally, recruiters and employers take you more seriously, and this will result in more job opportunities and higher-value job offers.

I have decades of experience in the human resource and recruitment industries, and have interviewed thousands of people and screened more than 50,000 résumés.

With sections on résumés, cover letters, interviewing tips, networking, direct marketing, salary negotiation and career goal setting, this book is the essential job-hunting career guide.

Tom O'Neil

AUTHOR'S NOTE

I use the word résumé as a generic term for curriculum vitae or CV. While a résumé usually means a shorter-form document in Canada and the United States, in most markets the three terms are used interchangeably, so when an employer asks for a résumé they are effectively asking for a CV, and vice versa.

All web resources and sites were checked prior to printing. The author and publisher can take no responsibility in cases where websites have changed or resources are no longer available.

WE ARE ALL BRANDS

THINKING OF YOURSELF IN A DIFFERENT WAY

THE NEW REALITY!

Over the last 30 years there has been a huge change in the way employee recruitment takes place. As well as this, the power of the individual to take control of their job hunt has increased massively.

We are used to the concept of 'brand' in products and companies. We buy a certain type of drink or wear a particular type of clothing, as it sends a message about the type of person we are. Corporate brands have dominated the 21st century, with names such a Coca-Cola, McDonalds, Toyota, Subway, BMW, Manchester United and Hugo Boss commanding a huge income due to the strength of their brand.

Historically, people who were considered 'brands' were usually famous singers, musicians, sportspeople, media celebrities and models. These were the people the general public adored and fawned over, emulating them in their dress, style and lifestyle.

Today the whole recruitment and job hunting world has turned on its head. Whether you are a student or CEO, you are now considered a brand (whether you know it or not), and the power of this brand will dictate how successful you are in your future career search.

Taking strong personal control of your brand, and leveraging it to increase your job hunting impact, is now pivotal to standing out against others in the international job market.

Organizations have a problem

An open job vacancy is a major problem for an organization. If a company is seeking to employ a Receptionist, they are stating that they don't have a representative to warmly welcome visitors and make them feel comfortable during their first impressions of the organization. In the short term this is inconvenient for visitors, and over the long term it displays a lack of professionalism.

An opening for a Sales Representative means that a business does not have all the sales resources available to sell their products within their chosen market. Over the short term this means they won't hit their sales budget, and over the long term they may lose market share to a competitor.

If the vacancy is for a CEO, the organization is stating that they are now lacking someone to give them strategic direction and a trusted representative for shareholders. Over the short term the business will lack a cohesive strategic path for the future, and over the long term they will lose overall value for their shareholders as their profits (and brand) plummets.

It's important to understand that the larger the responsibilities of the role and impact of the position, the bigger the 'problem' is for the employer.

As well as this, if there is enough work in an organization for five Office Administrators, and there is one vacancy, four people will have to do the work of five until a replacement is found. If this process to find a new Office Administrator takes too long, this will frustrate the four staff and another may leave, leaving three people to do the work of five!

Become the 'solution' to the employer's problem

It is vital to understand that the key to successful personal branding and job hunting is to become the 'solution' to the employers 'problem'. The more of a solution you appear to be to an employer's problem, the higher the chance of a successful interview and employment.

Personal brand is key in this process, as a strong brand equates to a more powerful solution for the employer. The more positive the 'brand' you carry, the more palatable you are to an employer hungry for a solution to their problem.

Becoming famous in your field

For a moment, imagine you owned a computer gaming business and you had two applicants of a similar background apply for the role of Game Designer. Both had the same qualifications and experience in your industry. Both worked for big name companies and have directly worked in the type of role you were advertising. The difference between the two candidates would be small and very hard to pick.

However now imagine that one of these candidates had a stronger 'brand'. For example the second candidate also hosted their own podcast on computer gaming that had 20,000 followers around the world. Imagine if that same person had also written a couple of articles for a gaming magazine and had been interviewed on local radio about a new innovative idea in the industry. Who is the stand out candidate now?

Sadly most people don't understand they are carving out a brand (either positive or negative) in their day to day actions and decisions at work. Consciously starting the process of developing a strong personal brand today, will pay off huge dividends in the future.

The better short term personal brand decisions you make today, will bit by bit create better job prospects and opportunities over your long term career.

YOUR PERSONAL BRAND AS AN INVESTMENT IN THE FUTURE

Becoming 'famous in your field', an 'influencer in your industry' or a 'celebrity in your space' is the new norm for many people wanting to jump ahead of their competition in the new and exciting international job market.

While you may not necessarily be comfortable with these terms and concepts within your industry, having a strong brand will ensure you are at the top of the pile when the recruiter calls!

Developing a strong personal brand is not something that happens overnight. However starting work toward developing a trusted name for timely delivery, knowledgeable service and high level of customer service will be a solid investment in your long term career.

What does your 'brand' say about you?

I would like to run an exercise with you. When you read the five brands over the page, I would like you to take 60 seconds to write down all the verbs and adjectives that represent the brand of that company to you. For example the automotive manufacturer 'BMW' may register words in your mind such as 'Quality', 'Fast', 'Innovative', 'Expensive', 'Efficient' or 'Luxury'.

McDonalds

Toyota

Subway Restaurants

Apple (the company not the fruit!)

Samsung

Now that we have determined that company brands have positive and negative verbs and adjectives that represent them and their business, do the same exercise with the people below:

Steve Jobs

Oprah Winfrey

Mother Teresa

Barack Obama

Richard Branson

'Like the world leaders above, you also have verbs and adjectives that represent you. Take five minutes to now write down the verbs and adjectives that you feel honestly represent you to your business colleagues, friends and family. Try very hard to be authentic in this exercise, we all have positives and negatives in our professional and personal lives.

Me

Another way you can get some very good feedback about the words that best represent your brand is to ask someone you trust to give you honest and fair feedback using the exercise above. Remember that this exercise can be quite painful if you don't feel some words are relevant to you, so choose a person who you can be totally honest with.

After you have completed this exercise, analyze the words that genuinely represent your positive and negative attributes, as well as your strengths and weaknesses.

Ask yourself the following questions:

- Which words are you most proud of?

- Which words are ones you would you most like to change?

- Which words would you like to add to your list in the future?

- What can you do, learn, study or sacrifice to gain these words in your 'brand list' in the future?

DIFFERENCE BETWEEN 'BRAND' AND 'REPUTATION'

While they are both tied very closely and seem almost identical, there is a small, but important distinction, between brand and reputation.

Your reputation is the total sum of your words and actions (both positive and negative) up to this point in time. To a large extent, 'reputation' is historic, and is based on how you have treated others, successes you have achieved, expertise you have gained and the things you have said and done (both on and offline) in your life.

You have a different reputation in the world depending on who is viewing you. Your parents, brothers and sisters, friends, business colleagues, clients and potential employers will all have a different perception of your reputation based on what you have achieved in your life and how you have acted around them.

'Brand' on the other hand is something that is more future focused, and points to your ability to deliver a certain outcome in a reliable and positive manner. For example, while the consumer electronics firm Apple has a strong reputation for innovation and quality products (historical), their brand tempts people with the promise of exciting new products and they are prepared to spend 48 hours outside a store to be the first to purchase the product (future). In the same way, your reputation gives a potential employer trust in your abilities, while your personal brand gives them further confidence that you will continue to operate at this level in the future.

Remember that both reputation and brand are highly vulnerable to bad news, and a poor choice (even if it is unintended) will very quickly erode the hard work you put in to get a strong reputation and brand.

WHAT DO YOU WANT TO BE DOING IN 10 YEARS' TIME?

As a professional career specialist, one thing that truly perplexes me is that people in general do not do any planning (or even thinking) about their long-term (or even medium-term) career.

Sadly these people jump from job to job every two to three years or so, making a reactive choice to move on when they don't get on with their boss, feel they are not being valued or when their job has lost its challenge.

At this stage they then play 'Job Lotto', gambling their future career on vacancies that just happen to be open that day. When they are successful in their application, they then move to a new company, form new relationships, lose contact with old friends, and on more extreme occasions, move city or even country.

This random (but highly common) approach is certainly not the best way to manage your long-term career plan. As well as this, if you don't focus on developing a clear personal brand message over the long term, your brand will be diluted as you jump from job to job and industry to industry.

A great way to start to gain a solid understanding of your long-term brand is to ask yourself the following two questions:

Exercise

1. What do I want to be doing for a career in ten years?

In terms of this first question, think about the mechanics of your answer:

- What type of job you would like to have?
- Do you want to employed full time, part time or on a temporary contract?
- Do you want to work for someone or be self-employed?

- Where are you based for work? (i.e. Do you want to live in the same area you work in now, or move somewhere else)?

- Will you travel much in this role?

- Will you work independently, or work with a team?

- Will you have staff responsibility, and if so, how many staff members would you like to directly manage?

After you gain a general understanding of the type of position you would like to see yourself in ten years time, ask yourself the second question:

2. What do I want to be known for / respected for in ten years time?

In terms of this second question, think more about:

- What types of things are you most passionate about?

- If you were 'famous in your field' or an 'influencer in your industry' in ten years time, what would this field or industry be?

- What can you do to start to develop a strong brand over the short term that would help you become 'famous in your field' or 'an influencer in your industry' over the long term?

DETERMINING YOUR BRAND VALUES

As mentioned earlier, having a strong brand is an ongoing journey, where your decisions, actions and words must consistently match your values.

Sadly, many people don't have strong brand success, as they continually do and say things that undermine their core brand and personal message. Therefore it's vital to determine the core values you stand for, and will not bend from. Once you understand and make these your own, making better long term choices will come naturally, and comprising situations and opportunities will become far and few between as people understand the depth of your brand.

Exercise

List below 15 to 20 values that you feel you can authentically make your own. These will help you to make positive career decisions that create an enduring reputation and strengthen your brand, creating more positive opportunities as you progress in your chosen vocation.

An example list may look similar to this:

Honesty	Social justice	Resilience
Empathy	Dependable	Life long learning
Loyal	Accountable	Consistent
Flexible	Innovative	Creative
Humorous	Ethical	Motivated
Positive	Optimistic	Collaborative
Passionate	Courageous	

It's vitally important to know the values that matter to you and those which you are prepared to fight for throughout your career. To paraphrase Dr. Gordon Eadie "If you don't stand for something, you will fall for anything."

The importance of your brand

As you can see, developing the fundamentals of a strong brand as early as possible is very important in job hunting. It is never too late to start putting some thinking into your long term career and to make a plan about where you want to head in the future. To quote a Chinese proverb *'The best time to plant a tree was 20 years ago. The second best time is now.'*

SELLING YOURSELF TO EMPLOYERS

WHAT DOES THE RECRUITER WANT?

Once you understand that you are a brand, it becomes quite clear that you now need to sell yourself effectively. The fact that the people dealing with staff are called the Human Resources Department says it all: **You are a RESOURCE.**

Because you are a resource, you must sell yourself. Think of yourself as a product. What makes this product stand out from its competitors? What is this product's unique selling points? What makes it better than the other products?

As a former recruiter and human resources management consultant for Deloitte, I was continually in contact with candidates who had significant potential, vying for positions. However, many could not demonstrate how they had added value to previous or current employers, and this meant they failed to convince me that they should be interviewed or recruited.

The problem is that most people have no idea how to actually 'sell and market' themselves effectively to potential employers. They do not realize that when job-hunting they become a 'product'.

For example, imagine if the world's number one golfer presented their résumé like this:

Occupation	Golfer
Responsibilities	Hit ball
	Hit ball again
	Tap ball lightly
	Tap ball into hole

Would this sell them as the world's number one golfer? Certainly not.

Another example could be selling an expensive Ferrari. You do not put an advertisement in the Cars For Sale section of your local newspaper with the text:

> Car, 4 wheels, engine. Goes. $100,000.

It is important that you 'sell' the features and benefits of the car to maximize interest in it (and to justify its price). Therefore, the advertisement should read something like this:

> Ferrari 360. 2006, low miles. 560 horsepower, top speed of 300 km/h. Racing red. Only $100,000. Live the dream.

When looking for a job, you must remember you are about to sell one of the most important products you can ever imagine. That product is YOU. From the start, you must have the same mindset about selling yourself as you would selling an internationally renowned product or service.

So, we have established that you are the product when job hunting. Now you must see yourself as an expert salesperson, selling this wonderful product.

You must know what you can offer an employer and what sets you apart from the competition. *Remember: If you only say what you get paid to do, you are only as good as everyone else.*

The fundamentals of employment are changing massively

The job world has undergone a radical transformation over the last 50 years. Gone are 'jobs for life' and with it the security that brings. A funny example of this is when I was completing a redundancy support course for a range of government employees, some of whom had been with the same company for 40-plus years. One older manager told the group that he originally wanted to be a land surveyor. As a young job-hunter he diligently went to the government offices, where he was told to register his interest on the fifth floor. He got off, by mistake, on the third floor, and spent the next 20 years as an accountant, only breaking into land surveying after half a career life had passed.

With the advent of the internet, contracting, job-sharing, and working from home, the United States Bureau of Labor predicts that the average young person in the United States will have about nine jobs between the ages of 18 and 32. That's one job every 18 to 19 months. Craig Rispin, a business futurologist, goes as far as to say that all jobs will be freelance in the future.

When I started working in recruitment 20 years ago, being in a job for five years was thought to be about the right amount of time. Today, that same period of time says to a potential employer that you have got stale and are afraid of a new challenge.

Do not let this worry you, however, if you are working in a role you enjoy for an employer you really like. Do not jump ship just because you think it is the right thing to do for your career.

Employers are not interested in you

Remember that an employer is not initially interested in you as an individual. An employer is only interested in getting the right person for the job.

When a company advertises a vacant position, they are not giving away money for the fun of it. They have to be judicious with the money that they have at their disposal, and be fully accountable to the company owners or shareholders for all the money they spend on employing someone.

On most occasions, a company advertises a vacancy for one of two reasons:

1. The company has grown, has gained more clients or sold more services and there is now more work to be done.

2. An employee has left the company and they must be replaced.

If a position is not filled quickly, the other members of the team will have to do the job of the person who has left. This will cause extreme frustration over the short-to-medium term, and lead to others leaving the company as they begin to feel overworked.

The vacancy becomes a 'problem' for the company, so the employer is seeking a 'solution'. It is vital that you tailor your entire recruitment approach as a solution specifically to the employer you are applying to. This means tweaking or tailoring your résumé and cover letter as well as paying particular attention to the key points employers and recruiters are highlighting in their advertisement.

Job advertisements

Generally speaking, recruitment advertisements take the following form:

1. Job title

2. What your key responsibilities are in this role

3. What the company seeks in a candidate

For example:

Customer Service Centre Supervisor

We are excited to start the search for a special person to lead our busy Customer Service Centre. The successful applicant will have previous experience and proven success in a customer service positions as well as excellent computer skills, the ability to thrive in a fast-paced environment and to lead from the front.

Duties and responsibilities will include:

- Supervising the customer service team of 4–5 staff
- Training and staff recruitment when necessary

- Reviewing and maintaining customer service records and forms
- Order entry processing
- Managing the daily workflow
- Resolution of customer complaints

We are looking for a great 'multitasker', someone who can build a rapport with customers and clients and has a 'can-do' attitude. You must also have proven leadership and coaching skills as well as excellent verbal and written communication skills.

The key here is to look at the final paragraph. There you find all the key skills, attributes and experience they are seeking. In this example the key 'solutions' for the employer include:

- Strong multitasking ability

- Excellent relationship development skills

- Proactive and 'can-do' attitude to work

- Demonstrated leadership and coaching background

- Very good written and oral communication and interpersonal skills.

It is important to 'mirror' these attributes in your résumé, cover letter and all your interviews to maximize your opportunity of being seen as the best solution to their problem—ahead of all other competing candidates. To be seen not as just another person sending in a résumé and hoping for the best.

The technique of 'mirroring'

Determine what employers are seeking in a candidate through evaluating job advertisements and position descriptions.

As mentioned earlier, in most job advertisements and position descriptions, there is a section entitled personal specifications/

characteristics. This section is the key to the role and this is what you need to target.

Read through the documentation and decide what the ideal person would look like. With your skills, achievements, qualifications and experiences, how can you meet or exceed these requirements?

Target the keywords and 'sell them back' to the employer

When a top, bespoke tailor makes a suit for a client, they take measurements to ensure it will fit perfectly. Remember to tailor your whole approach to the position for which you are applying. This will significantly increase your chances of reaching the interview stage.

Accordingly, you want to ensure that the main aspects and keywords in the advertisement or position description are 'mirrored' in everything you send and in your responses at any interview.

Recipe for success

Think about job advertisements and position descriptions as a type of recipe for success. As a former recruiter, when I advertised a position I effectively asked for a list of ingredients to make a chocolate cake.

'To be successful in this role you will need to have the following ingredients:

175 g butter

250 g of sugar

3 eggs

3 tablespoons of cocoa powder

125 ml boiling water

250 g flour

1 teaspoon of baking powder

200 g chocolate sprinkles'

The problem is that people don't look at what is required by the employer, and send their cover letter and CV stating 'I have the following ingredients to make a chocolate cake:

250 g of bacon

4 cups of cheese

1 egg

4 ml cold water

40 ml milk

1 birdcage'

Obviously the match is not there and the recruiter will instantly move on to the next candidate.

If an advertisement states that an employer is seeking an 'honest and focused individual', you might state in an interview that you are a 'person with integrity, who focuses on setting and achieving business goals'.

Other examples include:

- Honest or possessing integrity
- Customer driven or client focused
- Proactive or keen to pursue new opportunities
- Team player or works well in a group
- Autonomous or self-directed
- Hands on or practical

Become the solution to the employer's problem.
This is what will get you the job.

Remember—the job hunt is a race. But unlike the Olympics, there is no prize for coming second. Only disappointment and wasted time. Therefore, work hard on becoming the employer's solution, and you will gain your next role in record time.

THE MAGIC WORD IS 'RESULT'

Your job in a job-hunt is to come first! Most résumés list a host of general responsibilities one does during one's career; however, what really gets an employer excited is the 'results' that came from those responsibilities. Demonstrating the 'results' you achieved throughout your career makes the decision to recruit you easier, because it gives the employer what they want to see and highlights what sets you apart from all the others trying to get that role!

Avoid cluttering the résumé with unnecessary personal opinions and unsubstantiated comments such as 'hardworking', 'honest' and 'creative'. Employers want evidence of your performance record and you will get the chance to highlight these 'results' in the Major Achievement sections of your résumé.

Other comments to avoid include such things as:

- 'Significantly increased database of clients.'
- 'Visited eight potential clients per day.'
- 'Sent direct mail to 10,000 possible new clients.'

These statements are not what the employer needs to read— they do not describe quantifiable results.

To make the three statements above more useful and better suited to the purpose of attracting the attention of a potential employer, you could expand them as follows:

- 'Increased database of clients from 150 to 300. Result: Doubling turnover in the territory over a two-year period.'
- 'Visited eight potential clients per day. Result: The ratio of sales produced to calls made was one in four. The average

sale was ... and consistently averaged two sales per day, or ... per week. After three months, sales had increased by 50 percent compared to the previous incumbent's performance.'

- 'Sent direct mail to 10,000 prospective clients. Result: This promotion campaign converted into 360 sales at a total of ...'

This gets the reader's attention and makes you more attractive as a prospective employee.

DISCOVERING YOUR ACHIEVEMENTS AND HOW TO EFFECTIVELY 'SELL' YOURSELF TO EMPLOYERS

The O'Neil Major Achievements Questionnaire (OMAQ) helps individuals to discover their key career and personal achievements. It is published in the 2008–2015 editions of the world's best-selling career guide *What Color Is Your Parachute?* and has been translated into more than ten languages.

The OMAQ tool helps you to discover both your career and personal achievements, giving you tangible examples you can highlight in both your résumé and at the interview.

It is vital you know not just who you are, but also how to market yourself in a way an employer can easily understand. The easiest and best possible way is to define your achievements in a quantifiable and ordered way, demonstrating what you have achieved in the past. This, in turn, will show what you are capable of in the future.

O'NEIL MAJOR ACHIEVEMENTS QUESTIONNAIRE

The O'Neil Major Achievements Questionnaire helps candidates methodically discover areas of achievement (results) in their career and personal life, which they can include in their résumé as well as draw on in interviews. This questionnaire takes time to complete (from 30 minutes to two hours), but the answers could well mean the difference between your getting or not getting that next job offer.

Think of your working and personal experiences and the skills you believe you have learnt. Which ones are you proud of? What things have you done in your career that few other people have achieved? In your résumé, assign these achievements to both the company and the position in which you worked.

It is important to be quantitative when you do this—for example, mention specific dates, percentages, monetary values, brand names etc. But remember that it might not be appropriate to reveal potentially confidential information to prospective employers. A good question you could ask yourself is: 'Is this information common knowledge within the industry or is it commercially sensitive?'

Key questions to ask yourself

Education

- Did you win any awards for study or gain any scholarships?
- Did you have any high (A or above) individual or overall grades? If so, what were the papers and grades?
- Were you involved in any committees etc?
- If you are a recent graduate, detail the courses you have completed for your qualification.

- Did you work while you were studying? If so, did you receive any promotions or gain any achievements in the role?
- Were you involved in any competitions or projects that were successful?

Sales / Account management

- Have you consistently exceeded your set budget in a role? If so, by what percentage or monetary value?
- Have you exceeded your set budget in a particular month/ quarter? If so, by what percentage or by what value?
- What level are you compared to in regard to the other sales professionals in your company? (For example, number 3 out of 20 in the sales team)
- Have you increased market share? If so, by what percentage or value?
- Have you brought on/gained any major clients?
- What major clients are/were you responsible for managing and selling to?
- Have you managed to generate repeat business/increased current business? If so, by what percentage or value?
- Have you won any internal/external sales awards? This could include trips abroad or prizes.
- Did you develop any new successful promotional/ marketing ideas that increased sales?

Administration / Customer services / Accounts

- Did you set up or improve any systems and/or processes?
- Did you take any old administration or paperwork-based systems and convert them to an IT-based system or App?
- Was there a quantifiable difference in the company/

business unit from when you first joined to when you completed the project or left the business?

- Did you assist in reducing customer complaints etc?

Event / Logistical management

- Have you managed any major suppliers?

- Have you been involved in any major logistical or relocation projects?

- Have you organized any events or conferences? If so, how large were they (both people attending and total budget if possible) and where and when were the events held?

General

- Did you have any performance targets you had to achieve? Did you consistently meet these or exceed them?

- Were you promoted? If so, in what years and to which roles?

- How long have you spent within an industry? For example, 12 years' experience in the fashion industry.

- Extra authority awarded after a period of time within a role? (For example, began as a Receptionist but after three months was awarded with further clerical responsibilities including data entry and accounts payable.) Note that commonly these responsibilities awarded to you do not affect your job title or salary.

- Have you led, or been part of any projects? If so, what was the goal, budget and timeframe? What was the result?

- Have you been asked to take part in any trainee management courses/management development programs?

- Have you dealt with any regional or overseas branches, operations, suppliers or customers?

Positive feedback

- Did you receive any business, community or other awards? (For example, acknowledged for support/service of clients/staff etc.)

- Have you ever received a 'very good' or 'excellent' performance appraisal for a certain period of your employment? If so, in what year did this take place?

- Did you receive any written or verbal client/customer/ managerial commendations/ letters of praise?

- Can you think of any occasions where you gave excellent customer service and how did you know the customer was satisfied? (What was the outcome? How did it benefit the company?)

Responsibility

- Have you been responsible for the purchase of any goods/ services in your business? (For example, air travel/PC acquisition.) What was your purchasing authority limit?

- Have you had any budget responsibility? If so, to what level? (For example, responsibility for divisional budget of $200,000 per annum.)

- Have you had any staff responsibility? If so, to what capacity/how many staff were you responsible for, both directly and indirectly?

- Were you responsible for any official or unofficial training? If so, what type, for whom, and how many people have you trained? (For example, responsible for training 12 new staff members in all customer services aspects, as well as in the in-house computer system.)

- Were you responsible for any official or unofficial coaching/mentoring of staff?

- Have you been awarded responsibility for inducting new staff members?
- Have you been responsible for any aspects of recruitment? (For example, writing the job advertisement, screening, interviewing, verbal reference checks etc?)

Memberships

- Do you hold memberships to any industry bodies?
- Have you been a representative on any committees? (For example, a health and safety committee.)
- Do you belong or have you belonged to any professional clubs, voluntary or otherwise?

Mechanical / Print / Technical

- What machine or systems experience have you gained?
- Are there any special truck/car/marine machine brands that you have serviced, maintained or repaired?
- Have you commissioned or set up any production lines/machinery at work?

Voluntary / Community / Unpaid work

- Have you completed voluntary or unpaid work for any organization or company? (For example, a church, school, community service, special needs organization.)
- Have you taken part in any leadership roles, and if so, to what extent?

Building / Construction / Trades

- What major projects have you worked on? How much was the value worth? (For example: Reception refurbishment – ABC Bank Head Office, $1.2 million.)

- Have you been involved in training apprentices
  or inducting new team members

Project Management / IT / IS / Software

- What systems, software, and hardware
  experience do you have?

- What ICT brands have you serviced, maintained
  or repaired? What software have you utilized?

- Have you developed any websites, apps or software?
  If so, what were they, and did they positively affect
  the business? What was the successful outcome?

- What major projects have you led or been part of?
  What was the project goal, budget, methodology (e.g.
  PRINCE2) and timeframe? What was the result?

Published / Presented Work / Social Media

- Have you had articles, papers or features published in
  hard copy or online, in any magazines, journals, books,
  blogs, podcasts etc? If so, what publications and when?

- Have you developed a strong social media
  brand either personally or for an organization?
  What social media tools did you use?

- What social media tools/platforms are you skilled in?

- Can you highlight any success you have had in
  developing networks or generating high levels of
  online engagement (e.g. Facebook likes) or traffic?

- Have you presented any topics at any conferences or
  completed any public speaking? If so, what subjects have
  you talked about and how large was the audience?

- Have you been a representative of
  an organization in any way?

Language Skills

- List all the languages you know.

- For each, qualify your level of expertise. Include terms, such as fluent, conversational, basic, limited etc.

To assist in drawing out your achievements

If you are having trouble working out your achievements, complete this task below for each role, starting with your current position and working backward.

S—**Skills** (What skills did you learn in this role?)

E—**Experiences** (What experiences did you have?)

A—**Achievements** (What achievements did you gain?)

L—**Link** the relevant aspects to the job you are applying for.

Remember to use a strong achievements focus when you imagine your future employment. Think about how you can add value in the future. For example:

- Get involved with special projects outside your main job

- See how you can improve systems

- Help with training new staff in PC systems you know well

- Keep track of your commendations

Actively hunt out new opportunities to complete achievements that can then be used effectively when you apply for future roles.

Moving forward into employment

The information you generate by answering the above questions will also be handy during performance appraisal time because it will allow you to demonstrate in a quantitative way what you have achieved in your role. This could well assist in improving your overall performance rating and increasing your annual bonus or salary.

DEVELOPING YOUR RÉSUMÉ AND COVER LETTER

GETTING YOUR BROCHURE OR RÉSUMÉ RIGHT

Your résumé is your brochure to the employing world. As specialist résumé writers, we have seen many amazing examples of poor spelling, crazy details and general written incompetence from all sorts of job-seekers. Examples of what not to do include:

- Not supplying a name, telephone or email contact details. This generates a problem if the employer wants to call the person in for an interview.

- Quote from a résumé: 'The meek and the mild will be the rungs to the ladder of my success.'

- Fundamental spelling mistake: 'Company— ABC Consulting. Position—Analist.'

- A person spelt their first name wrong at the start of their résumé in a large font size.

- Quote from a résumé: 'Some time we need to go to the customer's horse to help them set up they computer and network.'

- On one occasion, an HR professional who should have known better sent in a 39-page résumé. This résumé had 10,700 words (that's about 40 percent of the words in this book!).

- My personal favorite: 'I am a stickler for detail as in any contract environment the devil is in the details and a good project manager must appreciate the need to ot the I's and cross the T's.'

Companies spend millions of dollars creating professional brochures to market their products to their target audience. Your résumé is your brochure—it must 'sell you' to employers just as a travel brochure sells travel to an exciting location. It must highlight the key points that meet the employer's requirements. In addition to this, it must be brief, i.e. have enough information to sell you within two to four pages.

DIFFERENT SECTIONS OF A RÉSUMÉ AND THEIR PURPOSE

A successful résumé would always include most of the sections detailed below. The following order is also important because you are trying to guide the reader on a journey. First, you must highlight yourself as being a 'solution', then demonstrate the results and achievements you have gained throughout your career, reinforcing the fact that *you are the one* they should be interviewing.

Objective

The Objective has been described as the 'soul of the résumé' and appears immediately after your name and contact details. It instantly informs the assessor on what you require in a work role. If this is done well, it will give the impression that you are a focused person who knows what they want in life. This is always a good look.

The Objective is an important statement in gaining the attention of the employer. Put as simply as possible, the aim is to show what you want and what skills you have to help you get what you want. This makes it easier for the employer to decide if you meet the needs of the company.

The Objective needs to be brief and to the point. For example:

- The role that you are seeking.

- The key skills/qualifications that you can bring to the position.

If you can tailor your résumé directly to the role, your potential employer will see at a glance whether you are someone they can use or just 'another résumé'.

Sadly, a significant percentage of résumés received are discarded because the employer cannot easily identify the applicant's requirements. Tailoring a résumé makes the reader's job easier. If you can do this, you have a much higher chance of progressing to the interview stage.

If you tailor a résumé to a company name or industry (which I suggest), always be careful that you change the Objective when you apply for another position. Human resources managers always grimace when they see a résumé that has an objective for another company on the résumé. You do not want to pitch your résumé at a possible competitor.

Good examples include:

OBJECTIVE

Seeking the role of sales representative with ABC Realty, where a successful business development and account management background within the realty estate industry can be utilized.

Seeking the role of quantity surveyor with ABC Company, where strong estimating and quoting experience within the construction and building sectors can be utilized.

Remember when writing your objective to always have the employer's needs in mind.

Personal Summary

The Summary is effectively the front porch of the career house. If it is not well presented then no one will want to enter. The employer could make incorrect negative judgments or, even worse, stop reading your résumé altogether if the first paragraph is not right.

The Summary is just that—a summary. It should be easy to read at a glance, contain the highlights, and spark the employer's curiosity and desire to know more about you.

To make certain the employer quickly feels you are on the same wavelength as themselves, highlight the required skills they detail in their advertisement and match yours accordingly. Using the mirroring technique mentioned earlier, ensure the key words the employer is seeking are incorporated into the summary to make sure you stand out among the other candidates.

Use short sentences/statement paragraphs and bullet points. Allow space around your bullet points to ensure that they stand out. For example:

Personal Summary:

- Office management professional, degree educated, with strong experience within the customer services and administrative environments.

- Results driven, with a business-minded approach to office management, which resulted in rapid promotion within current company.

- Acting as a role model and leading by example led to acquiring a mentoring and training of staff role shortly after joining present company.

- Excellent communication and interpersonal skills with the ability to relate effectively and professionally to people at all levels in a company.

- Acknowledged by management for high attention to detail and ability to manage numerous projects simultaneously.

- Proactive and positive team member, with a 'can-do' attitude to all projects.

- Recognized for operating effectively in fast-paced and pressured environments.

- Quick to learn new principles and concepts, with a strong focus toward ongoing learning and personal development.

Personal Attributes / Quotes

Take quotes from previous employers, customer references, commendations, appraisals etc and include these in the résumé. For example:

PERSONAL ATTRIBUTES

I found Peter's biggest strength is his ability to create, implement and monitor processes ... He also displayed a determination to succeed and was able to build an excellent rapport with the rest of our team members and stakeholders ... Peter has always shown himself to be completely trustworthy, reliable and an extremely hard worker ...
He is respected by myself and all who know him and is of complete integrity and honesty.

Lisa Abbey, Operations Team Leader—Microsoft Corporation

Using personal quotes is a very effective way to demonstrate 'soft' competencies (i.e. team player/great communicator) in a tangible way. This is also how you gain 'instant credibility' and give the recipient confidence to proceed.

Career History

The 'Career Funnel'

An employer's interest in your career history is generally as follows:

Period	Employer's interest	Key responsibilities
Last 5 years	Very interested	4–6 bullet points
5–10 years	Quite interested	2–4 bullet points
10–15 years	Slightly interested	1–2 bullet points
15–20 years	Somewhat interested	1–2 bullet points
20+ years	Not interested	General statement

You should therefore give relative detail in relation to these periods. The more interested in a period the employer is, the more you want to inform them of your responsibilities by providing greater detail. You also want to make the section brief and easy to read, so present the information in clear bullet points.

Remember, the employer is most interested in your *latest* role. The positions you held when you had just left school are the least important. This is why your career history is sequenced with the latest or current roles coming first then working backwards to least recent (The Career Funnel).

If you are uncertain about how to describe your responsibilities, visit a recruitment website or job board and identify a position that is similar to your role. Using this as a template, describe your duties clearly. For example:

2012–Current   LAND MANAGEMENT LIMITED,
　　　　　　　　　PROJECT LEADER

Key responsibilities:

- Define project scope, goals and deliverables
  that support business goals in collaboration with
  senior management and stakeholders.

- Effectively communicate and manage various
  project management timelines, processes and
  methodologies with customers and internal staff.

- Coordinate project plans for cross-functional teams.

- Develop project plans and status reports as well
  as comprehensive commercial documentation.

- Serve as the key contact and communications
  point for the projects.

- Estimate the resources and participants
  needed to achieve project goals.

- Identify and manage project dependencies and critical paths.

- Track and report project tasks, activity,
  documentation and time tracking.

Major achievements

Under each position (not company because you may have
been promoted within one company), highlight your major
achievements to demonstrate the success you have had in this
position. For example:

Major achievements:

- Successfully exceeded all 'work unit per day' targets.
  On occasion, exceeded targets by up to 45 percent.

- Using strict project management methodologies,
  successfully led the delivery of key projects on
  time and within budget. Examples include:
  - Managed a $1 million project to assess, design and
    deliver a solution for customers in remote areas.
  - Developed and implemented a new delivery system
    that reduced overall logistic costs by 12 percent.

- Developed and implemented a number of effective systems to streamline administrative and IT operations within the department. Examples include:
  - Set up a new IT system (APD Pro) to successfully monitor new work practices, both internally and onsite.

- Received numerous customer and managerial commendations for providing a consistently high standard of surveying support and service.

- Awarded further responsibility for training new and current staff in survey process procedures as well as internal systems.

Qualifications and Professional Development

Key qualifications should be included in your résumé. These include degrees and diplomas.

Standard courses should also be included, if they are relevant. However, obscure courses or courses that may not have much appeal to an employer should be left out.

For example, if you are applying for the role of Office Administrator, you would include the relevant qualifications and courses you completed. For example:

- Bachelor of Business Administration— State University (2014)

- Microsoft Word Certificate—Institute of Learning (2010)

- Time Management for Administrators—ABC Training (2009)

- Customer Service Fundamentals—A Training Centre (2007)

Computer Knowledge

Unless you are an IT specialist, only highlight the key software programs you can use. If you are an IT specialist, you would look to include this after the Personal Summary section at the start of the résumé to draw strong attention to these skills and knowledge. If you are not an IT professional, this section tends to sit after the Qualifications and Professional Development section.

For example:

- Experienced in using Microsoft Windows, Word, Excel, PowerPoint, Adobe Acrobat and Google docs as well as a variety of in-house software packages.

Personal

Including personal details in your CV gives the employer information about yourself. However, it is important to include only details that can be perceived as positive. What's acceptable to include in this section has changed considerably over the years. In fact, this is the section most employers will not ask you about as they fear breaking Equal Employment Opportunity law.

Feel free to include, or not include, any of the following. Only include details on these if you think it increases your chance of gaining an interview:

- Marital status

- Health

- Non-smoker

Voluntary Work

This section tends to be left off general résumés. However, it can give insight into a person's community spirit as well as demonstrate responsibility and personal development outside of the work realm. This section is focused on actual voluntary experience you have completed. For example:

Voluntary work:

- Involved in a number of community
  support programs including:
  - Collector for various animal welfare appeals (2009—2014)
  - Member of the School Board of Trustees (2012—Current)
  - Church Board Member (2013—Current)

Published Work / Presentations

Highlighting any published work or presentations you may have made at conferences can reinforce your standing as a specialist in these key areas.

Interests

Although this may seem irrelevant to your professional life, your interests and hobbies can say a lot about you as a person. For example, team sports indicate a team player in the workplace. Someone who enjoys reading may have keen intellectual interests. Try to ensure that you come across as a healthy, well-rounded person, without bending the truth.

Verbal Referees

Ensure that your verbal referees know potential employers are going to contact them about your suitability for employment. It is always embarrassing if this does not happen and the referee is taken by surprise. Let your referees know when you start your job hunt and be sure to gain their approval prior to them being contacted. This will give your referees an opportunity to more accurately remember you and your performance before they are contacted, which could result in making their reference very positive.

You generally need two to three professional referees, and these should not include relatives or friends.

Having referees in your résumé can speed up the interview process. For example, if an employer is very keen to employ you and can complete the verbal references in one day, a job offer could hopefully follow next.

Referees also add credibility to your approach. Include your referees' names, positions, companies and contact details, which may include a mobile number, a land line and an email address.

What **NOT** to put into your résumé

Always remember that a résumé is your brochure. It is therefore crucial that you have a long hard think about what you do and do not include. Ask yourself these questions:

- Is the information positive and in line with what the employer is looking for in a future employee? (i.e. 'Mirroring' your application)

- Does it show the benefits of an employer hiring me?

- If required, does it show that I am either a 'profit opportunity' or a 'cost benefit' to the company?

A résumé is not a disclaimer

While you must not lie in your résumé, you want to ensure that you are shown in a favorable light. (See 'Damage control')

Check out: www.cv.co.nz/templates for a free MS Word résumé template.

SAMPLE RÉSUMÉS

Assistant Accountant

John is an Assistant Accountant with five years' experience in the business software and real estate industries, in a variety of accounts roles. Through hard work, he was awarded further IT and finance responsibilities in his current position, and has a solid knowledge of a wide range of accounting legislation and systems.

John Smith

159 Hope Drive, New Town, 01234

Mobile: (0123) 456 7890

Email: jsmith777@email.com

OBJECTIVE

Seeking the role of Assistant Accountant with ABC Business Services, where strong financial and business administration qualifications and experience can be utilized.

PERSONAL SUMMARY

- Proven experience with accounting legislation and systems, including taxation, auditing, fixed assets, accounts payable/receivable and financial accounting.
- Willing to learn new accounting and financial principles, with a genuine focus toward ongoing professional development. Passion to become CA qualified in the future.
- Solid background using a wide range of systems including MYOB, Quicken, MS Excel, SQL Server, MS Access, Customer Relationship Manager (CRM) and MS Outlook. Excellent keyboard skills.
- Excellent communication and interpersonal skills, with the ability to develop strong relationships at all staff levels.
- Qualifications include a Bachelor of Business (majoring in Accounting & Commercial Law)—State University.

PERSONAL ATTRIBUTES

John launched into his role with enthusiasm and professionalism that had both myself and my partner impressed. John has contributed new ideas and improvements to our practice, as well as introducing new clients to the business.

Brian Andrews, CEO—Innovative Business Systems

CAREER HISTORY

Jan 2013–Present Innovative Business Systems

- Commenced as an Accountants Assistant.
- Due to a professional and quality-first approach, awarded with further senior-level financial and IT management responsibilities.

Key responsibilities:
- Oversee financial and accounts management for the business.
- Manage accounts payable/receivable and follow up debtors and credit control.
- Complete invoicing and reporting.
- Professionally handle debtor queries.

Major achievements:
- Developed and implemented a number of effective systems to streamline administrative operations within the business.
- Provided key input into the development of a major accounting system implementation for ABC Ltd. Identified the internal control weakness in the current system and recommended changes.
- Received numerous customer and managerial commendations for providing a consistently high standard of support and service.

Mar 2009—Dec 2013 Systemz Real Estate Ltd,
Accountants Clerk
Key responsibilities:
- Complete general book-keeping and accounts using MYOB.
- Oversee invoicing and debtors reconciliation.
- Manage credit control and debt collections for the business.
- Organize and coordinate sales budgets.
- Liaise directly with clients regarding finance terms and accounts.

Major achievements:
- Demonstrated strong practical skills in prioritizing, multitasking and time management as well as the ability to work autonomously.

QUALIFICATIONS AND PROFESSIONAL DEVELOPMENT
- Bachelor of Business (major in Accounting & Commercial Law) —State University (2009)

INTERESTS
- Interests include tennis, film and current events.

COMPUTER KNOWLEDGE
- Windows, MYOB, Quicken, SQL Server, MS Access, MS Word, Customer Relationship Manager (CRM) and MS Outlook.

REFEREES
- Brian Andrews, CEO—Innovative Business Systems
  Mob: (555) 123 6738
- Julie Wildon, General Manager—Systemz Real Estate Ltd
  Mob: (555) 123 8901 Email: julie.wildon@system.com

Sales Representative

Brian has worked in both the UK and Australia in the sales industry. He was promoted from Sales Administrator to Sales Representative in 2010 and has been very successful achieving and exceeding challenging sales targets in his current position.

Brian Kumar

2/22 Anderson Street, Oaktown 125 831

Mobile: (021) 555 5555

Email: kyr2@email.com

OBJECTIVE

Seeking the role of Sales Representative, where a strong background in business development and key account management can be utilized.

PERSONAL SUMMARY

- Business development professional with a proven background in successful sales. Focused on achieving set targets and business goals as well as delivering a high standard of customer service.
- Logical and analytical thinker, with a strong problem-solving approach to work. Displays initiative when seeking solutions and makes sound business decisions.
- Excellent communication, interpersonal and negotiation skills, with the ability to develop strong relationships and influence.
- Self-motivated and disciplined with a determined attitude to succeed.

PERSONAL ATTRIBUTES

Brian gained the team's trust very early on and was always ready to extend his help to all team members. Brian is also able to work on his own while meeting deadlines set out ahead of him and produced very good results. External relationships were also key to his role, which he managed with integrity at all times.

Ann Smithe, Sales Manager—ABC IT Systems

CAREER HISTORY

Jun 2012—Present ABC IT Systems

- Commenced as a Sales Administrator
- In 2013, promoted to the role of Sales Representative.

Key responsibilities:
- Build and maintain strong relationships with corporate clients and identify opportunities to increase service offerings.
- Identify potential clients and implement effective strategies to gain their business.
- Lead and facilitate business and sales presentations.
- Develop strong corporate networks within the local region.
- Proactively solve any issues directly or indirectly involving customers and the sales process.
- Ensure monthly targets are exceeded and the regular call cycle is maintained.

Major achievements:
- Successful at achieving and exceeding set key performance indicators (KPIs) and business development targets.
- Due to a professional and client-focused approach to work, developed a loyal client base as well as strong referral and repeat business.
- Awarded further responsibility for training new and current staff in quality-based customer services and sales techniques as well as internal systems.

Sep 2008—May 2012 Digital Audio Ltd, Retail Sales Consultant

Key responsibilities:
- Meet monthly sales targets set by managers.
- Provide a consistently high standard of service to a diverse range of customers.
- Complete high-volume cash and credit handling.
- Sell high-technology products and solutions as well as develop strong relationships with both businesses and individual customers.
- Merchandise and display new stock effectively to drive further sales.

Major achievements:
- Recognized for performance excellence and superior customer service skills through feedback and surveys from customers.
- Successfully demonstrated the ability to work in team-based environments and to tight deadlines.
- Provided a high level of support and coaching to new team members.

QUALIFICATIONS AND PROFESSIONAL DEVELOPMENT
- National Diploma in Business—University of Technology (2010)
- Advanced Sales for the IT Sector—Tom Hopkins Training (2009)
- Sales Success—Dale Carnegie Training (2009)

INTERESTS
- Interests include personal development, golf, cooking, theatre and socializing with family and friends.

COMPUTER KNOWLEDGE
- MS Windows, Mac OS, MS Word, MS Excel and MS Outlook.

REFEREES

- John Bridges, Sales Manager—ABC IT Systems
  Mob: (555) 777 1234
- Lisa Maxwell, General Manager—Digital Audio Ltd
  Mob: (555) 888 1298

Junior Chef

Janelle graduated with a Diploma in Culinary Arts in 2010 and has a real passion for developing a strong career within hospitality. With four years' experience in the industry, she has been awarded further responsibility for training, mentoring and coaching other team members in the kitchen.

Janelle Anderson

188 Simpak Road, Eden Park, N17 0AA

Telephone: (09) 570 5555

Mobile: (027) 888 5555

Email: JA1988@email.com

OBJECTIVE

Seeking role as sous chef where both qualifications and accomplishments in culinary arts, as well as special talent for food preparation can be utilized.

PERSONAL SUMMARY

- Genuine passion for food, with a commitment to developing a strong career within this challenging and exciting industry.
- Excellent skills in food preparation and solid practical knowledge of:
  Budgeting/planning
  Stock management
  Menu development
  Kitchen hygiene
  Health and safety
  Food nutrition
  Food technology
  Cooking methods
- Strong communication and interpersonal skills with the ability to relate effectively and professionally to people at all levels.

- Proven ability to multitask, a high attention to detail and able to work to deadlines.
- Proactive and positive team member, with a 'can-do' attitude to all projects.

QUALIFICATIONS AND PROFESSIONAL DEVELOPMENT

- Diploma in Culinary Arts (Level 5)—University of Technology (2010)

Papers:

- Information Technology for Culinary Arts
- Culinary Cooperative Education
- Kitchen Management
- Gastronomy
- Advanced Culinary Practices and Principles I & II
- Advanced Hot and Cold Desserts
- Advanced Cakes and Pastry
- Workplace First Aid—ABC Safety Systems (2010)

CAREER HISTORY

Feb 2012—Current Domus Café, Eden Park, Junior Chef

Key responsibilities:

- Train and mentor new kitchen staff.
- Prepare food using effective hygiene practices.
- Complete high-volume cash handling.
- Work flexible hours, within a team environment.
- Ensure compliance with company standards of product quality, service and cleanliness.

Major achievements:

- Received numerous customer and managerial commendations for providing a consistently high standard of support and service.
- Gained strong face-to-face customer services and communications experience as well as practical skills in prioritizing, multitasking and time management.

- Awarded further responsibility for training staff in kitchen systems as well as customer services.

COMPUTER KNOWLEDGE

- General office-related products include MS Word, MS Excel, MS PowerPoint, Internet Explorer, MS Outlook as well as a variety of in-house software packages.

INTERESTS

- Interests include cooking, travel, walking and reading.

REFEREES

- Bill Williams, Lecturer—University of Technology
  Telephone: (555) 777 1234
  Email: billwilliams1965@email.com
- Haresh Singh, Manager/Owner—Domus Café
  Tel: (555) 545 7777
  Mob: (555) 888 777

FINAL WORD

Never be afraid to be creative in your approach to a future employer. Years ago I ran a career development course where one woman proceeded to tell me that her untraditional résumé was very successful. We quizzed her further and she then showed me what she had done. Frustrated at the low degree of interest her old résumé was generating, she drew two stick figures to represent herself and her husband and wrote some basic details about herself.

After photocopying 100 of these, she distributed them randomly to businesses within the city center. Within a very short period of time a manager at a respected government department called her in and offered her a role immediately. He was taken by her desire to work hard as well as her creative and fun side, which was portrayed through her 'non-traditional' résumé.

Hello,
We have just relocated to the city.
My husband has a job—but I would like one too. My name is Joan and I am a mature woman with a great sense of humor. I have worked for various government departments, as well as the State Hospital, Lands and Deeds, Prison Service, GP Stationery and Local Polytechnic; all in admin roles, apart from the Prison Service. If you need a reliable, self-motivated person, please give me a call on the number below.
Thanks for your time.

I discovered another example in a newspaper that reported on a college graduate seeking her first public relations role. She sent three firms a shoe in a box with a note saying, 'I'm just trying to get my foot in the door.' The cheesy technique worked because she stood out from the crowd of other applicants.

At the end of the day, what's really important is to strike a balance between creativity and professionalism. If you can do this effectively, you will be remembered for the right reasons and get an interview.

COVER LETTERS—THE FRAME TO YOUR RÉSUMÉ

Publishers around the world spend millions of dollars each year designing covers to promote and sell their books. A well-crafted jacket will entice the reader to delve further into the book, hopefully leading to enough excitement that they then make a purchase.

In the same way, a good cover letter should 'frame' the résumé, providing an enticing introduction to read further and learn more about the candidate it is representing.

It is not necessary to have a long cover letter. At a recent conference where I was speaking, an HR Manager, two recruitment consultants and a general manager were asked by the audience how long a cover letter should be. The resounding response from these professionals came as one immediate answer: 'ONE PAGE ONLY!'

A cover letter helps in the following ways:

- It shows the employer that you have researched their company.

- It demonstrates your ability to communicate professionally in a written format.

- It is usually your first point of contact, so it can set the tone for your whole relationship with the company.

A recruitment friend of mine recently completed an analysis of the quality of cover letters sent to his consultancy. Out of every 100 candidates, on average:

- 73 percent of applicants supplied no cover letter or a brief introduction in the email of one to two lines;

- 16 percent supplied poor quality cover letters with spelling mistakes and highlighting no relevance to the specific role being advertised;

- 11 percent provided a professional cover letter highlighting the key aspects from the advertisement and their relevance to the appointment.

Therefore, according to these figures, by just creating a professional cover letter, you can immediately position yourself in the top 11 percent of candidates right from the start.

Interestingly enough author Tony Beshara in his career guide *Unbeatable Résumés: America's Top Recruiter Reveals What REALLY Gets You Hired*, asked hiring authorities from a variety of industries and roles the question, 'How important is a cover letter when you are receiving résumés?' Surprisingly of the more than 3,000 respondents, 86 percent said 'not very important'. Understand however, that if that is the case, 14 percent of potential employers and screeners think the cover letter is 'very important', and like the above, its quality will determine your success early on!

Don't play the odds. Every time you put any information forward about yourself or your application, make sure it is top class!

Rules for cover letters

- Write a different cover letter for every prospective employer.

- Always write the letter to a particular person, ensuring the recipient's name is spelt correctly. If you do not know the name or the spelling, ring the company to find out.

- State why you are writing.

- Indicate the title of the position.

- Explain your reasons for interest in the organization.

- Express your enthusiasm for the role.

- Communicate your motivation and strengths.

- Indicate how the employer can contact you.

- Check spelling and grammar.

Cover letter structure

The basic structure of a cover letter includes four sections. Avoid the temptation to record your entire career history in a cover letter—all this does is undermine your careful work constructing the résumé.

Section 1: Why you are writing

This should include the reason for your letter—that is, you want to apply for a specific position. It is important to state the following details to clarify the position you are applying for. The company may have more than one vacancy being advertised and you want to make sure you are considered for the role you want. Include:

- the title of the position, including any reference numbers;
- where and when it was advertised.

Section 2: Your core career and personal experiences

This section should explain what career and personal experiences you have to do the job well. For example, you could highlight specific positions from your career history that are directly relevant to the advertised position. This could also include a list of the key tasks needed to perform the role you are seeking and demonstrating that you have completed the requirements of the role very successfully.

Section 3: Your personal strengths

I discourage listing 'personal strengths' in a résumé because it is a factual document and there is no way to verify someone's personal strengths. However, in a cover letter, this is acceptable. Cover letters are personal letters of introduction, so highlighting personal strengths are not out of place.

Use this section to bring to the fore your strengths, personal qualities and qualifications, showing how they have benefited previous companies and explaining the value you can add to the new company.

Also outline what professional advantages you can offer the company if they employ you.

You want to ensure that the main aspects and keywords in the advertisement or position description are 'mirrored' within the cover letter. For example, if the advertisement states that they are seeking an 'honest and focused individual', you could place in the cover letter that you are a 'person with integrity, who focuses on setting and achieving business goals'.

Section 4: Your contact details

Let the potential employer know when and how they can contact you. If you can't take calls during the day, let them know that they can contact you after hours on your mobile or by leaving a message. Ensure you include all your contact numbers at the bottom of the letter. If it is difficult to get hold of you, a potential employer may give up trying and you will miss out on the job opportunity.

Check your grammar and spelling and get trusted friends to also check it. Remember, as with your résumé, each cover letter should be written with one job or employer in mind. Tailor both your résumé and your cover letter to the employer and the position—do not recycle old cover letters or copy directly from previous résumés.

COVER LETTER TEMPLATE

Date

Contact details of the person you are writing to
Email/Postal address
Company

Dear *[contact name]* or *[position]*, *[if you do not know this,
write 'Dear Sir / Madam']*

I wish to apply for the position of *[position name (Reference
Number XXXXX)]*, which your organization recently
advertised. Please find attached my résumé, which highlights
my achievements associated to the areas of *[insert relevant
areas]*.

  Currently I am employed by *[XXXXX]* as a *[XXXXX]*. Some of
my key responsibilities within this role include:

-
-
-

  Prior to this, I have been employed within / I have enjoyed
a strong career within *[provide one-sentence general
summary]*.
*[For example: Prior to this, I have a strong career within business
administration, finance, banking and customer services.]*
  I believe I have proven throughout my career that I am *[use
keywords from the job description or advertisement]*.

Or:

I believe I have demonstrated during my time with *[company
name]* … .

Or:

My personal skills/strengths include *[list these]*.
I am qualified *[add qualifications relevant to the job]* which I
believe would provide a solid foundation for this position.
I hope to have the opportunity to discuss this exciting
position further with you. Please feel free to contact me on
my mobile, or on my home telephone number after hours, to
answer further questions you may have about my application.

Yours faithfully, *[your name]*
Phone:
Mobile:
Email:

SAMPLE COVER LETTERS

Cover letter example (business)

21 October 2015

Steve Mills
Human Resources Manager, ABC Company

Dear Steve,

I wish to apply for the position of Client Relationship Manager, which your business recently advertised. Please find attached my résumé, which highlights my achievements associated to the areas of key account development, project leadership and financial management.

Since 2013, I have been employed as a Business Manager and Consultant at Business Control Systems Limited. Some of my key responsibilities in this role include:

- Leading relationship management with key stakeholders and agencies;
- Managing all financial services, including monthly reporting, budget setting and statutory reporting;
- Supervising the operations of three retail outlets with a turnover of $8 million per annum;
- Overseeing development and operation of all IT systems and administration.

Between 2009 and 2013, I was employed by Relevant Technologies. Commencing as the Contracts Manager, I was promoted in 2010 to the role of Business Support Manager. Key aspects of this position included developing, implementing and managing all contracting processes, including service specification development, documentation and training.

I believe I have proven throughout my career that I have a number of key skills and attributes that meet the requirements of this role. These include:

- Excellent communication and relationship management skills, with the ability to develop trusted relationships with customers, business partners and stakeholders;
- Strong IT and MS Office literacy, as well as solid database knowledge;
- Proven written and verbal skills, with the ability to produce highly professional management reports;
- Strong time management skills, well organized and the ability to work successfully to deadlines;
- Flexible and enthusiastic team member, with a 'can-do' attitude to all projects;
- High level of perseverance and the ability to influence and persuade.

My qualifications include a Bachelor of Business Studies (majoring in Accounting), which I believe provides a solid foundation for this role.

I look forward to discussing this exciting opportunity further with you. Please feel free to contact me on my mobile or on my home telephone number after hours to answer further questions you may have about my application.

Yours faithfully,

Joan Smith
Telephone: (09) 555 5678
Mobile: (021) 555 1234
Email: joansmith121@email.com

Cover letter example (student)

21 October 2015

Steve Mills
Human Resources Manager, ABC Company

Dear Steve,

I wish to apply for the position of Helpdesk Administrator, which your organization recently advertised. Please find attached my résumé, which highlights my qualifications in Information Systems and e-Commerce.

   I am passionate about developing a strong career in the IT field. I have recently completed a Bachelor of Commerce & Administration (with a double major in Information Systems and e-Commerce) at the University of New Town. Some of the key papers I completed during this degree include:

- Information System Development
- Advanced Project Management
- Strategic Information Systems Management
- e-Commerce Principles
- Advanced Database Management & Programming
- Internet Design & Development
- Advanced Topics in e-Commerce

In addition to this, I have gained solid work experience in a number of customer services and sales roles during my studies.

   I believe I have proven throughout my career that I have a number of skills and attributes which meet the requirements of this role. These include:

- a genuine passion for the IT environment, with a positive approach and a 'can-do' attitude;
- desire to build my skills supporting network infrastructure, telephony platforms, production servers and client devices;
- quick to learn new principles and a strong focus toward on-going learning and personal development;
- proven ability to multitask, a high attention to detail and able to work to deadlines.

I look forward to discussing this exciting opportunity further with you. Please feel free to contact me to ask any questions you may have in regard to my application.

Yours faithfully,

Robert Jones
Telephone: (09) 555 5678
Mobile: (021) 555 1234
Email: bobjones333@email.com

Enhancing your chances

With regard to your cover letter, points that will enhance your employment chances are:

Sending your cover letter addressed to a specific person. The reasons are:

1. You can ring after a few days to see whether your application was received.

2. Phoning the addressed recipient will build up a rapport with them.

3. While talking directly you may find out whether there is an interest in your application or the person you are talking to may have some questions they can ask that will speed up the process.

4. You can follow up again and see how your application is proceeding.

Very important

Recruitment consultants are more likely to do something for someone who has contacted them and built a personal connection or rapport. Most applicants do not ring recruiters. They just send a résumé. Recruitment consultants appreciate the time taken by someone who gives them a call.

If you do not know the name of the person who is taking the applications, ring the company and ask. When you speak to someone at the company make sure you ask for the correct spelling of the person's name.

Check out www.cv.co.nz/templates for a free MS Word cover letter template.

LINKEDIN, SOCIAL MEDIA AND NETWORKING

UNDERSTANDING SOCIAL MEDIA AND NETWORKING

As anyone can plainly see today, social media is an enormous force for professional personal branding, job hunting and career management.

With a multitude of platforms available to 'sing your praises', the success of the next vacancy you apply for, may well be based on how positive (or negative) you are perceived to be online.

Surveys providing a correlation between social media and recruitment practices vary widely. However, employer surveys show that up to 93 percent of recruiters actively use social media as a key screening tool.

As many people are prepared to put the 'real them' on social media for all to see, recruiters and human resources professionals will use this information to ascertain their 'fit' in the business they are hiring for.

As this career guide is a basic introduction to personal branding, we will briefly touch on some of the key social media platforms to ensure you are familiar with the things you need to do to be perceived as a quality candidate.

LINKEDIN

Launched in 2003, LinkedIn is a well-established member of the social media family. Focusing primarily on business relationships and networks, it has become the leader in its category, with approximately 350 million members around the world.

LinkedIn is a terrific way to promote your personal brand to key players and influencers in your industry. As well as this, executive recruiters trawl LinkedIn for quality candidates they can 'head hunt' into choice appointments very quickly and efficiently.

The true power of LinkedIn as a legitimate selection tool was demonstrated to me when I was once surprised that a highly successful media friend did not have a LinkedIn profile. Mentioning to her the importance of successful personal branding and its link to the platform, she responded that she had originally set up a profile, but took it down as she 'was getting too many job offers'!

Having an 'achievement' focus in your profile

While many people see LinkedIn as an 'online résumé' it is so much more than that.

As discussed in Section 2, it is important to sell your achievements, not just your responsibilities, to gain interest from an employer. Too many LinkedIn profiles are either only partially completed, or are a list of the person's responsibilities.

If your CV is your 'brochure', so LinkedIn should be your 'online brochure' demonstrating your true value to potential employers and networks.

Due to changing text limits in LinkedIn text fields, it is important you focus on 'outcomes' not 'inputs' for each of your career roles in your profile. Instead of concentrating on a list of seven responsibilities for the role of Sales Manager, focus your profile to highlight your key achievements in each role.

This will ensure you are seen as a quality candidate with strong accomplishments and successes, rather than a candidate who is just as good as everyone else in a similar role.

Word of warning:

Remember that LinkedIn is to a large extent an 'open' forum, allowing a diverse range of people internationally to read confidential information about you and companies you have worked for. Therefore I suggest you never share financial data and use only percentages to highlight your competencies.

For example:

- Don't say: Successful in increasing business turnover from $10 million to $12 million within six months.

- Do say: Successful in increasing multi-million dollar business turnover by 20 percent within six months.

Building a quality network

The temptation when joining LinkedIn is to try to get as many connections as possible, highlighting your influence to other members, as well as developing a wide community that you can leverage in the future for job hunting and business opportunities.

However, like going up to complete strangers in a party, quickly introducing yourself and then rushing off to make a new 'contact', most LinkedIn members get turned off by the 'be my friend' syndrome.

Just like in real life, its far better to have 220 quality contacts you can develop strong relationships with, rather than 2,200 contacts who are not authentic.

The judge of a good LinkedIn contact is 'could I help this person at some stage in the future to develop their business, knowledge or career, and in return would they also be able to assist me reach my goals?

To link up with another person, you must have something in common with them. This stops random people 'spamming you' and trying to develop relationships that are not naturally present in some limited capacity. To link up with a person, you simply click on the 'Connect' button and choose one of the options. These normally include:

- Colleague

- Classmate

- We've done business together

- Friend

- Other

- I don't know 'Person Name'

If you are choosing any but the last option, this helps to ensure you have a genuine relationship or reason to connect. The selection 'I don't know 'Person Name'' leads to an automatic message stating that this is not actually an option to connect.

Other ways to link up with someone is to choose the drop-down arrow and click on 'Get introduced.' This then analyses your relationship network, and gives you the option to contact others who are linked to the person, providing you with the option to ask them to make an introduction on your behalf.

However if you purchase a paid membership to LinkedIn you receive a set number of 'InMail' messages that allow you to contact the person directly, without a network connection.'

The Approach

Another key point is how you approach people to connect with them. Instead of using the standard wording that pops up when you start the process:

I'd like to add you to my professional network on LinkedIn.
—John Smith

Find a way to engage further, so the recipient understands the contact is genuine and authentic. A great way to do this is mention how you know them or why you feel the connection is beneficial to you both. For example:

Hi Steve,
I saw you speak last week at the National Insurance Brokers Conference and I really liked your point about 'personal branding'

and how I can use this to increase my conversion rate. I would be really grateful if I could add you to my professional network on LinkedIn.

Kind regards,

Tom O'Neil

The importance of groups

After developing a strong LinkedIn profile and reaching out to link up with your network of industry colleagues and friends, the next stage is to join relevant groups in your interest field.

I suggest a two pronged approach here:

1. Firstly join all the relevant groups in your career and interest space. Remember however, the more groups you join, the more 'clutter' you will receive in your inbox. This creates its own problem as you won't have the time to follow all of the posts properly if you belong to 50 groups. Better to follow ten groups than get swamped with email and read nothing from 50 groups.

2. Of these, chose two or three 'key' groups where you would like to develop influence and authentically promote your personal brand.

These key groups need to have a number of aspects if your brand promotion is to be successful. They include:

Numbers

A decent amount of people in your group. Joining a group of five people is not going to extend your reach very far.

Focus

Narrow group focus. Joining a group that has a very wide interest base, rather than a more specific focus will mean less people will be interested in something you post. While your insightful comments about the latest steel prices may be a great read, most people in a general group will not be interested. However, those in the 'Steel Manufacturers and Processors' group will more likely be interested to read what you have to say.

Open vs closed

Closed groups tend to be better to develop a personal brand within. An open group means anyone with a LinkedIn account can instantly join and start posting their thoughts. Therefore the quality of comment in the group may be compromised by people who do have not have relevant experience or knowledge to add genuine value.

However there is a barrier to entry for closed groups as you have to demonstrate a specialized knowledge base, worked in a particular industry or have reached a certain level in your career to justify inclusion. When you initially click to join the group, your pending membership is assessed by the group moderator and they decide whether or not you are suitable for inclusion into the group.

As you can understand, this means that only people with the above qualities can join, make comments and take an active part in discussions.

Activity

The last sign of a quality group is activity. If you see a group that has had little or no postings in the last few days, or if there is a lot of action but it is dominated by only a couple of people, these factors probably point to the fact that the group is 'dead' (or at least snoozing…)

How to become an influencer in the group

After you have joined a couple of key industry or job type groups that you want to influence, start to slowly develop relationships and link up with other like minded people in the group.

Try a find the groups 'groove' by looking at consistent posters and key messages that come through. Once you understand these things, start a strategic plan to develop your influence.

1. Reply to posts within your key groups

No matter who you are, when someone likes something you do or say, you can't help but think positive things of them.

Therefore read the posts of other members, and when you find a post you like or has an insightful point included, press 'Like', then 'Comment'. Write what you like about the post or what you learnt from it and thank the author for bring it to your attention.

Two things happen here: Firstly you are responding to the post in a professional and positive way which will encourage the author. Secondly your name (your brand) will be associated with that positive comment. As you sprinkle positive and insightful comments through the group, your name will start to be seen and recognized by key influencers and your own influence (and personal brand) will start to increase.

Warning—Be careful not to post wonderful comments on every post that pops up as the opposite will start to happen. You will be perceived as a non-genuine person who is just trying to 'be seen'. Make sure that your comments and responses are authentic and you can stand by every single one you post.

2. Post your own comments

After you have a good grasp of the type of discussions that take place in the group, write some of your own posts. Be careful to do solid research and refer to facts and figures from trusted sources. Remember you are now 'putting yourself out there' and are open to comment, criticism and even attack from others in your group. Try very hard to not take negative comments personally (it's something that takes a bit of time to learn), instead be humble and always respond to the comments in a positive and professional way, even if you don't feel like it.

Remember you need to protect your brand, so starting a slanging match between yourself and another member of the group means there will be no winners. Just horrific entertainment from those you are trying to make a positive impression on! Sometimes you need to lose a battle to win a war.

3. Reference studies and other articles

This is by far the easiest and most powerful way to demonstrate your value to group members.

Spend some time researching interesting online articles through high profile industry websites. These may be specific to your group (such as online trade journals) or general newspaper or magazine style sites (such as the *Harvard Business Review*, *The Economist*, *Financial Times*, *Time Magazine*).

When you have found an interesting and insightful article that would add value to your group, post a link to the online story and then write a short statement introducing it and asking for feedback from other members.

If this is done well enough, it can start a feeding frenzy of group interest, with key influencers providing comment and deep discussion taking place on- and off-line.

The best part is that you are then perceived by the members as someone who obviously spends a lot of time researching the industry and adds a terrific amount of value to the group as a whole.

Why is developing a strong brand in key LinkedIn groups important for job hunting?

Understand that if you have spent a decent amount of time developing a strong personal brand in your key groups, the people who will be recruiting your next role will probably also be a member of these groups. Therefore when your CV crosses their table at some stage in the future, they will remember your name in a positive way. Your strong personal brand will mean you are perceived as an excellent candidate as they already know you are an influencer in their industry!

Recommendations and Endorsements

Having a strong list of endorsements and recommendations can really add value to your personal brand on LinkedIn.

Recommendations

A recommendation is when someone who has worked with you, or knows you well, submits a paragraph about your skills and talents for others to read.

Most of the time these are very positive and can be used to highlight your value to your network, as well as to candidate hungry recruiters and HR teams.

A good way to start the recommendation process is to recommend a range of people yourself first.

This is easy enough to do. Find a person in your contact list who you would like to recommend and then go to their profile page. To the right of the 'Send a message' box is a small dropdown arrow. Put your cursor over the arrow and then select 'Recommend' from the expanded list.

It is then an easy process to write a positive referral, talking about how you know them, what is was like working with them and highlighting some of their key skills.

Warning—It is vital that this is done in an authentic way and your comments are genuine. It does you no favors to provide recommendations for others if you are not prepared to stand by them in the future.

The great aspect about this process is when the recipient receives your recommendation, they then are given the prompt 'Would you like to complete a recommendation for *[Your name]*?' On many occasions human nature kicks in and they feel guilty if they do not 're-pay the favor'. Therefore you will hopefully receive one in return!

You can also directly ask your connections to write a recommendation of you for your profile. Go to your LinkedIn homepage and again place your cursor to the right of the blue button reading 'View profile as'. Select the link for 'Ask to be recommended'. From here, select the role you wish to be recommended for, then choose up to three people to ask.

Endorsements

Endorsements, like recommendations, demonstrate the level of skill your community believes you have across a diverse range of competencies and skills you highlight about yourself.

When you set up your profile you can list up to 50 skills that you would like to have other members endorse. Tailor your skills list to the type of role you are seeking and what you want to be known for as a professional in ten years' time. (See Section 1) This will ensure you are not stuck with a strong skill endorsement for 'MS Word' if you are a CEO.

Again, like recommendations, only genuinely endorse people with skills you know they have. I continually have people from all around the world endorsing me for skills they would have no way of knowing my competency in. Sadly that in turn damages their brand as someone who is not wholly truthful.

When you endorse a person (the process is very similar to

how you recommend people), again the opportunity for them to endorse you pops up. Therefore a quick way to gain a solid amount of endorsements yourself is to endorse as many people as you genuinely can.

Remember however that the level of endorsement for a particular skill a person has, is not reflective of the level of skill they genuinely have in real life. It's only a reflection of their ability to convince others to tick the right box!

Job Hunting

A large amount of companies are now using LinkedIn itself as their main recruiting tool to advertise their vacancies.

Job hunting on LinkedIn is simple as it has an integrated job board that can provide you with suitable jobs that meet your set criteria when they are advertised.

The first time you use the LinkedIn job tool, you develop a profile by selecting the area, industries and job level you wish to apply for.

Once this is complete, you can search by job title and apply for exciting new opportunities. Remember if you find a job on the LinkedIn job board, chances are your LinkedIn profile (and probably other social media) will be carefully studied by the recruiter and Human Resources team. Therefore, make sure your profile is top notch to ensure you stand out to your best of your ability!

Recruiters

Recruiters love LinkedIn as it allows them to head-hunt and cherry-pick top candidates who would otherwise not be seeking new opportunities in the recruitment market.

The good news here is that as so many LinkedIn profiles are of such poor quality, when you invest the time to design a professional profile that 'sells' yourself effectively, you automatically stand out against your competitors when recruiters come calling!

LinkedIn Paid Services

LinkedIn also offers paid premium services for job hunters, as well as those who wish to get the most out of the website.

Their 'Job Seeker' option includes:

1. Three 'In Mail' messages, allowing you the opportunity to contact anyone on LinkedIn, even if you're not connected.

2. You can see who has recently viewed your profile and how they found you.

3. You become a 'Featured Applicant' and automatically advance to the top of the recruiters' applicant lists.

4. You also receive 'Applicant Insights' allowing you to view how you rate against other candidates.

Because the investment is relatively small and as it will give you a slight edge in the competitive employment world, this is certainly something I suggest you purchase.

NETWORKING THROUGH OTHER SOCIAL MEDIA: TWITTER, YOUTUBE, BLOGGING AND PODCASTS

In terms of job hunting, it is best to imagine social media as a large network. Everything you do online will impact on how you are perceived by an employer.

This can work well if you have a good social media presence and you are leveraging your social media profile to inform others that you are on the job hunt.

LinkedIn is very dominant in the job hunting space, while the other media tools play a supporting role.

The great thing about social media is that it allows your family and friends to look for job opportunities on your behalf.

In many organizations the HR team will attempt to recruit employees in-house through friends and family first, prior to advertising in the common market. This then allows your contacts who work in these organizations the ability to give you a 'head start' and allow you to apply when the pool of potential candidates is quite small. Therefore for this reason alone, it is very important to let your social media contacts on Facebook, Google+, Twitter, Instagram, Tumblr, Flickr, Pinterest, Meetup, Vine etc. know that you are now available and seeking a new and exciting opportunity. Obviously you'll need to be discreet if you are still employed at this stage as you don't want to flag to your current employer that you are looking elsewhere.

Twitter

Twitter is the leading short format social networking service that allows users to send and read short 140-character messages named 'tweets'. Created in 2006, Twitter rapidly became part of our social framework, with more than 300 million active users.

Twitter is a great way to get your 'brand' message out in a positive way. For example, if you are a passionate environmentalist, and you are wishing to pursue a career in this area, you should be tweeting about things that matter to other environmentalists. Subjects you may want to tweet about could include the latest research on global warming, habitat destruction, pollution, deforestation or local environmental issues.

As a Human Resources Advisor, specialist areas you may tweet about to develop your brand could include talent management, improving recruitment systems, succession planning, industrial relations or changes to employment law.

Of course when recruiters follow up to determine your suitability for a specific role, they will find a history of tweets from a committed and passionate environmentalist or human resources professional, which will only add to your overall employability.

This also works for a wide range of industries including fashion, design, HR, finance, law, sales etc. At the end of the day it's about building a respected personal brand platform for the long term.

YouTube

YouTube is a media sharing website that allows people to quickly and conveniently upload videos to the internet. Founded by three friends in 2005, YouTube has more than 800 million unique users every month.

Like Twitter, YouTube allows you to profile your brand, sharing what's important to you and sharpening your message to the world. This may include your own short videos, profiling of videos that support your core message, and ultimately, the creation of a channel dedicated to promoting your field of interest (and your brand).

Making your own videos and creating your own channel can be a very powerful way to strengthen your employability, leveraging also into book and TV deals etc.

The key to a strong brand on YouTube is not necessarily high quality production (however this does help of course), but providing strong value to your audience. Think about the questions they have, and provide direct answers to their problem.

As a strongly visual medium, many people love YouTube as it puts a 'face to the name' of the specialist and gives more credibility than just anonymous tweets and blogs. As well as this, by building up a solid base of interviews, teaching videos and so on, you provide a great 'library', highlighting yourself as a leader in your field.

Similar sites that also allow you to develop a following include Vimeo, Metacafe and Indestructables.

Blogging

Arguably the oldest of the social media platforms, the concept of blogging is very simple—writing online and searchable articles allows you to develop a strong and loyal following, as well as interact directly with your audience.

Following in the footsteps of international bloggers such as Seth Godin and Perez Hilton, you too can elaborate further on your Twitter posts, providing far more depth and detail in the areas you wish to share on your blog.

Blogging is also very Google friendly, allowing positive search results for your name (your brand) to be near the top of the page when a recruiter goes online to find out about you.

Articles about your area of specialty, interviews of interesting people you meet and sharing 'up to the moment' insight and research about a particular topic, all help you be seen as a leader in your field.

Podcasting

While they are quite niche, Podcasts have a huge following for those who enjoy them. Podcasts are usually an audio recording of you reading out your blog or article, giving the listener the opportunity to respond via email and social media. It's a social media medium that allows you to develop an audio channel to express your thoughts and promote yourself as an expert in your field.

Allowing listeners the opportunity to listen when they are in rush hour traffic, mowing the lawn or doing the dishes, Podcasting gives your audience a passive way to receive your content.

I am amazed at how quickly you can develop a strong following using podcasts, with many podcasters gaining thousands of subscribers within the first year of starting.

If being famous(ish) in different parts of the world may not be something that excites you, understand that the world is now a global marketplace, so your next employer may literally be sitting on the other side of the planet and hear your podcast that convinces them you are the team member they are seeking.

MERGING SOCIAL MEDIA

Each post, video, tweet, blog and podcast you put online creates a strong personal brand that dramatically increases your employability. Imagine if you were hiring a chef for a restaurant, and the first applicant had their own YouTube channel dedicated to teaching French cooking, a well-read international blog, and regularly tweeted interesting cooking facts to their audience, while the second applicant had none of these... who would you select to work in your kitchen?

Think about how to maximize your social media presence; you might write a post for LinkedIn, post it in your blog, record it for your podcast, and then promote it though Facebook, Google+ and Twitter. That way you consolidate your efforts to produce a very strong and cohesive message about your brand for recruiters and HR specialists to follow when researching you.

Using social media to minimize negative search results

Another good reason for developing a strong social media presence is if you have something negative in your history online, developing a positive history over time will push the negative result further down the page where a recruiter may (hopefully) not look!

Having a strong brand platform through whichever social media platforms you choose, should soon lead to a direct approach from a prospective recruiter or employer. The good news is they will probably have a positive opinion of your skills and abilities as your personal brand has already started doing its job defining you as an influencer in your industry.

Once you start working on a social media platform, ensure you continually check to see if people are trying to contact you through them. I know myself that I didn't check my Facebook account for a number of weeks, and found that I had missed over 30 messages that had come to me through that platform.

Remember that your online brand must match your offline brand too. Business speaker and author Justin St Vincent believes you are your own 'broadcast tower' emitting positive or negative brand influence into your world. A great example of the importance of offline branding was when an HR executive was pushed and sworn at on a train to work by an impatient commuter. A few hours later, that impatient commuter walked into an interview with the HR executive and didn't even recognize the man he had yelled at earlier that day. Of course he did not get the job! Consistency out in the 'real world' is vital if you are to capitalize on your hard work blogging, podcasting and tweeting.

INTERVIEW BASICS AND TECHNIQUES

WHAT ARE INTERVIEWS ALL ABOUT?

While we all think that employers are seeking the 'best person for the job', sometimes they are seeking the 'least risky' person for the job. Therefore all questions recruiters and HR staff ask during interviews come down to two fundamental points:

- Can you do the job?
- Will you fit into the team culture?

Their job is to assess you against the key aspects of the job and company—that is, to judge your skills and abilities and make their recommendation to the employer.

They assess your future potential from your past experience. This is why it is VITAL to know your achievements and what you can offer the company.

Dealing directly with a company, the interview process usually takes place over two to three interviews:

Interview 1: Can you do the job competently?

Interviews 2 and 3: Can we work with you as a person—will you fit our culture?

Being prepared is the key

To ensure you present at your best, you must be prepared. *A large percentage of the time the most suitable person for the available role does not get the position.*

The candidate who is best prepared will gain the role on most occasions. If you have an understanding of the prospective business—that is, you know how big or small the company is and understand their particular needs—you will appear to have more understanding in the employer's eyes and will be more likely to get the job over other candidates with greater experience who turned up for the interview unprepared.

The person that is most prepared is a person who:

- has a well-structured and tailored résumé

- knows about the company and its products

- has strong verbal references for the recruiter to contact

- has good questions to ask about the role and company

They will appear to be the best candidate (even though they may not have the best qualifications or experience), and they will get the job.

PASSION—THE UNDERUSED TRUMP CARD

A very underused, but highly effective, technique to gain the job of your dreams is to demonstrate your passion and enthusiasm. Passion drives us to achieve more in all areas of our lives and calls us on to bigger and better things. As Oprah Winfrey says, 'Passion is energy. Feel the power that comes from focusing on what excites you.'

If you get to an interview, but realize that you are deficient in a key area (for example, you do not have a specific degree or the direct industry experience that the employer is seeking), it is even more important to demonstrate your passion for the role or industry.

For example, while I have a strong background across many industries, I have spent no time in the marine sector. However, if I applied for a role in that industry, I could point out the fact that I have 15 years' sailing experience, spent three years as the vice president of a Yacht Club and own a 30-foot racing yacht. While this does not point to my direct knowledge of the sector, it demonstrates my genuine passion for the marine area and tells potential employers that this would not be 'just a job' for me.

If you can communicate this passion effectively to an employer, they may well choose you over a more qualified candidate with ten years in the sector who showed no real interest in the position other than it will pay them a salary.

TYPES OF INTERVIEWS

If possible, try to find out what sort of interview you will be going into prior to turning up. It is harder to focus if you are expecting a one-on-one interview and then find you are being grilled by a panel of six.

The main purpose of this process is to give the interviewer(s) a chance to assess your suitability and for you to demonstrate your personality, skills and abilities.

It is rare to only have one interview prior to receiving a job offer. Most employers interview their candidates between two to four times to be sure the candidate will not only be able to do the job but will fit well into the company culture.

The STAR method

The STAR method (Situation, Task, Action, Result) is an excellent way to answer questions where the interviewer is seeking a specific example to a question they pose. For example:

> 'Give an example of a time you went beyond the standard
> requirements to assist a customer. What did you do
> and how did you know the customer was satisfied?'

You should answer in the following way:

> **Situation:** Give a quick overview of the environment
> in which your example took place in. Include the
> company/organization you were working for and

your position. This situation is usually taken from a previous role you have worked in. However, use volunteer experience, or a relevant life event, if you do not have a suitable employment example.

Task: Outline the main issue you needed to solve and what you needed to accomplish. Remember to provide a specific incident or experience, not a generalized description.

Action: Describe in detail exactly what you did and actions you took when responding to the situation. Even if you are discussing a group project or setting, describe what you did—this is what the interviewer is seeking.

Result: Describe the positive outcome of the situation. What happened? How did the event end? What did you accomplish? What did you learn?

If you have trouble answering behavioral questions, think about it like telling a story: what happened, who was involved, and how it ended.

Face-to-face interview

This is the most common situation and takes place with a recruiter or manager interviewing you. Ensure that you listen to the interviewer well and engage them in the process. Make positive eye contact and use appropriate body language.

Attempt to establish a positive rapport with the interviewer and show them that your skills, abilities and personality will benefit the company. Do not over-reach, however, or seem too familiar.

Panel or committee interview

In this situation, you are faced with between three to seven interviewers. This is a great opportunity to highlight your presentation and interpersonal skills in a group context.

Try to assess the individual personality types of each interviewer and meet their needs. Engage with each person at their level. Before the interview you may be told who the panel will comprise of. If possible, do some research on these people through the company's website, as well as a business portal like LinkedIn. But again, do not appear over-familiar.

As you answer questions during the interview, keep your main eye contact on the person who asked the question, yet spread your answer and eye contact evenly amongst the rest of the panel or committee members. (For example, direct 40 percent of your eye contact on the person who asked the question and 20 percent on each of the remaining three interviewers.)

Try to find a 'happy smiler' on the interview panel, and keep referring to them during the process. When they smile at and engage with you, you will feel better and more relaxed, and will therefore perform better.

Behavioral interview or behavioral event interview

The Behavioral Event Interviewing (BEI) technique is when you answer an interview question giving real-life examples and facts from a specific situation. The key premise behind this type of interview is that your previous behavior is the main predictor of your future potential. Example questions include:

- 'Tell me about a recent goal you set and how you successfully achieved it'

- 'Describe a time when you were faced with a stressful situation that demonstrated your coping skills.'

- 'Give me a example of a time when you used good judgment and logic in solving a problem.'

- 'Tell me about a recent situation in which you had to deal with a very upset customer or co-worker.'

- 'Tell me about a time when you encountered conflict at work and how you handled it.'

- 'Tell me about a time when you have gone above and beyond to satisfy a particularly difficult customer.'

The interviewer is looking for specific answers. Identify things such as names, dates, places, monetary value etc. However, remember to not breach confidentiality with any current or previous employers.

Use the STAR method to answer these types of questions effectively. Or use the O'Neil Major Achievements Questionnaire to pull out examples of personal achievements and generate specific answers to these types of questions.

Telephone interview

Telephone interviews are increasingly used by companies as a key part of the initial screening process. A large amount of the time they are assessing your language skills and how you project yourself on the telephone.

You may find it easier if you stand up when you are being interviewed on the telephone. I find when I am talking with a customer or being interviewed for a news story, I stand up as this takes me away from any distractions and helps me to better control my voice and overall demeanor.

Treat a telephone interview as professionally as you would a face-to-face one. Prepare and prepare again.

Try to find a space away from distractions, such as co-workers, children or pets. Have a copy of your résumé in front of you so you can refer to it when required. This will also provide comfort during the process.

Focusing on the interviewer and their questions is the main priority during the interview. Use the same rules during a telephone interview as you would during a face-to-face interview (except, obviously, for eye contact and body language).

Group interviews

A group interview is when a group of people (say, four to ten) are asked to complete a task or come up with an idea together. Group interviews are designed to assess leadership potential within a body of people and the setting is usually somewhat informal.

Often there is a task to complete and the group as a whole develops a solution. Achieving a solution is not the goal of the group interview, however. The interviewers are assessing leadership potential and want to see how you relate to others in the group. Are you empathetic, friendly, a pushover, rude or aggressive?

Be friendly and agreeable in the group, yet stand by your convictions. Many people think if they steamroll over everyone else in the group, they will be seen as the key leader, not realizing they are being viewed by the interviewers as an arrogant 'know-it-all' who cannot work in a team.

Lunch / Dinner interview

Be careful in these situations. Although the setting is informal, you are still being judged as you would in any normal interview setting.

Use the interview to develop a positive rapport with your interviewer and follow their lead in what they eat and drink. If you do decide to drink something alcoholic, take small sips. Getting drunk will negatively affect your overall interview performance.

Please also avoid messy foods like spaghetti bolognese or barbecue pork ribs.

Competency / Criteria interview

These interviews are structured to reflect the competencies or attributes an employer is seeking for a particular position. These are usually detailed within the job specification or advertisement.

Make sure you have read the job description/advertisement in full and have a complete understanding of what the employer is seeking.

Prepare sample questions as if *you* were preparing to interview someone for the position. Once you have created these, collate sample answers that you feel would meet the competency requirements.

ACCURATELY READING THE INTERVIEWER

Allison Mooney, professional international speaker and author, details in her book *Pressing the Right Buttons – people skills for business success* the four key 'Personality Plus' types. She helps people think about who they are as well as understand who others are. This is highly useful for a candidate as it will allow you to 'speed read' the interviewer and give them the answers they need in a format they understand. The four key personalities are:

Playful
Look for:

- Stylish dresser. Bright and definitely eye-catching.

- Loud, talkative, relational, fun-loving.

- Smiley eyes, mixes easily, impulsive, wide body gestures, inviting.

- Extrovert and optimistic.

- Drifts in and out of conversations according to the interest of the content.

Environment:

- Messy and lots of pictures of friends socializing.

Listen for:

- The question—'Who?'

- Focus on relationships.

Respond to them through:

- Attention

- Approval

- Affection

- Acceptance

Powerful

Look for:

- Functional and power dresser.

- Strong presence. Decisive, fast-moving approach.

- Quick grab for control and no chit-chat.

- Direct and dominates the conversation. Has a self-confidence about them; may be restless.

- Talks about business competency.

Environment:

- Trophies and awards.

- Clutter, but they know where everything is.

Listen for:

- The questions 'What? and 'When?' They want results.

Respond to them through:

- Credit and appreciation

- Loyalty

Precise

Look for:

- Classic dresser and well-mannered.

- Thinker, organized and formal.

- Strategic approach, with organizational activity the highest priority.

- Selective listener.

- Talks about specifics and reasoning.

- Closed about their personal lives.

Environment:

- Charts/graphs, credentials.

Listen for:

- The question 'How?' or any relating to wanting more detail and facts.

Respond to them through:

- Sensitivity

- Space

- Silence and support

Peaceful

Look for:

- Comfortable clothing.

- Easy to be with. Relaxed, quiet and unflappable.

- Good listener and a calming approach.

- Sitting or leaning where possible.

- Measured with their gestures. Gentle.
  Environment:

- Old relics and keepsakes on desk. Family picture.

Listen for:

- The question 'Why?' They want reasons.

Respond to them through:

- Respect
- Harmony
- Value

Great questions to ask yourself during the interview to determine the interviewer's personality type include:

- Are they loud or quiet?
- Do they move with purpose and focus?
- What questions are they asking?
- How can I weave how they see the world into the conversation?
- Whether they are loud (probably Playful or Powerful).
- Whether they are quiet (Peaceful or Precise).
- Do they move quickly? (Playful or Powerful).
- Are they calm? (Peaceful or Precise).

As Mooney writes in her book, 'Remember to treat others as they want to be treated in the interview—not how you wish to be treated.'

HOW TO DEAL EFFECTIVELY WITH RECRUITERS

Recruiters are salespeople. Some of them will treat you poorly. However, do not allow yourself to be easily offended. This is sometimes hard as many recruiters will not return your email or calls.

Understand that they do not work for you—they work for the company. They, in fact, sell a product: you. If you imagine yourself as a car, your suitability depends on whether or not you as a car meet the requirements of the purchaser (the employer).

General things to remember:

- Recruiters are the 'gatekeepers' to many jobs. You must treat a recruiter with the same respect you would an employer.

- If you miss out with a recruiter, keep applying for any new roles they may advertise as they probably have forgotten about you and what you can offer. Recruiters also keep advertising new roles to gain new candidates and improve their talent pool.

- Understand that if you met with a recruiter two weeks ago, and they now have trouble remembering who you are over the telephone, they have probably interviewed between 40 and 80 new people and have read over 200 résumés in the meantime. Therefore do not take it personally.

- Keep in contact with recruiters and be positive and friendly.

- Do not only meet with one recruiter and then expect them to find you a job. The best recruiter in the world is only as good as the vacancies they have available and their contacts. Therefore spread yourself around between recruitment consultancies to ensure you are getting good coverage and exposure to employers.

- If you want to make a complaint at some stage about poor treatment by a recruiter, wait until you have a new job then make a complaint.

- On numerous occasions the recruiter will have very limited expertise in your field, and may be in their early twenties. While it becomes very easy to 'dismiss' this person for their lack of experience, they are the individual you need to develop a positive relationship with if you want to progress your application further. Until that time, do what they ask as they hold the key to meeting with the employer.

PSYCHOLOGICAL TESTING / PSYCHOMETRIC ASSESSMENTS

It is highly likely these days that you will be asked to complete a skills or psychometric test at some stage of the interview process. As a candidate, it is important to be fully informed about the assessment process you may well be experiencing. Ask the employer if there will be any tests, and if so what sort of tests you will be completing. Will there be a personality assessment (what sort of person are you?) or competency and skills-based assessments (numerical/written reasoning/MS Word etc.)?

Make sure you take a watch as some tests are done under time constraints to make them even more challenging to complete.

Numerical reasoning

In a numerical reasoning test, you answer questions using a range of facts and figures that are presented to you in a variety of ways. For example, a table, graph, series of numbers or associated tools. You are then given a range of questions and multi-choice answers based on this data.

Only one option is, of course, correct. You may want to use an extra sheet of paper and a calculator to work on the answer. Always ask whether a calculator is permitted in the test as you do not want to be seen as cheating.

Verbal reasoning

In a verbal reasoning test, you usually complete the answers by selecting something similar to the following:

A – True
(The statement is true based on the passage of information presented.)

B – False
(The statement is not true based on the passage of information presented.)

C – Not sure
(You are not sure whether the statement is true or false as there is no information presented regarding it.)

Personality questionnaires

Personality questionnaires assess your behavioral preferences in relation to your career and working style (for example, introvert/extrovert). They do not measure any specific abilities but attempt to assess how you view yourself, how you interrelate with others, how you problem solve key issues and how you deal with difficult circumstances.

Personality questionnaires come in a wide range of formats. For example, you may have to rate yourself against a set of specific requirements. In other formats, you may have to make difficult choices between different statements.

Generally speaking, there are no wrong answers. However, an employer could want a more extroverted person for a sales role and a more detail-focused person for a data analysis role.

Personality questionnaire example questions

Examples of the kinds of questions a personality questionnaire may contain are given in the box below.

Rate your response according to the following statement:
Select 1 – If you strongly disagree with the statement
Select 2 – If you disagree with the statement
Select 3 – If you are unsure
Select 4 – If you agree with the statement
Select 5 – If you strongly agree with the statement

1	I dislike meeting new people	1	2	3	4	5
2	I enjoy managing people	1	2	3	4	5
3	I am very creative	1	2	3	4	5
4	I get disappointed easily	1	2	3	4	5
5	I enjoy fixing things	1	2	3	4	5

How can I prepare effectively for psychometric testing?

Follow all instructions given by the administrator. If you don't understand something, ask the administrator immediately. One of my favorite assessments asked candidates to read a box of instructions on the first page, prior to starting the test. After three lines of general information, the instructions then stated 'This test is designed to ascertain how well you can read and follow instructions. If you read this, please turn the page over, sign your name and immediately leave the testing area.'

Candidates who did not read the guidelines didn't realize this assessment was effectively a trick, designed to ascertain whether a person actually read the instructions in the first place.

Any participants remaining would then go through and answer questions like 'If you were a fruit, what sort of fruit would you be and why?' It was always amusing giving this test to a roomful of candidates and watching one or two people immediately turn their test over, write their name and walk out, while the other 95 percent waxed lyrical about being oranges, apples, bananas and the like! Don't spend too much time on any one question. If you are struggling to find an answer, skip to the next one. On many occasions there will be tight time constraints, so it's vital to complete as much of the test as possible.

If you will be completing a numeracy-based assessment, ask if a calculator can be used. If not, you will need to quickly brush up on your manual mathematics skills.

Sit a range of practice tests online. The more familiar you are with different types of assessments, the more you will be prepared for whatever is put in front of you on the day.

Can personality tests be faked?

Many personality tests used in recruitment contain an internal checking mechanism to assess candidates' attempts at faking the results. On most occasions these can easily be picked up by a qualified assessor.

The more important question you should ask is why would you want to fake the results of a test? If you successfully changed your answers to meet the requirements of a sales position, for example, you may end up finding yourself in a job that you are not skilled in and do not like. If you are a quiet and introverted person, you will quickly find yourself becoming stressed with having to constantly meet challenging sales targets, perform cold calling, telemarketing and persuading people to buy products from you. At the end of the day, it is in your best interests to not try to 'tweak' your results.

While tests tend not to be overly fun to do (especially under time pressure), never moan or protest about having to do them. Everyone reaching the final stages of the process will have to complete the same test, so you only single yourself out as a potential troublemaker if you start to complain.

BE PROFESSIONAL IN YOUR RECORD-KEEPING

If you are regularly applying for jobs, all your hard work may well be lost if you do not take a disciplined approach to record-keeping. It is vital to know to where and when you sent all your applications. Set up a recording system (either on paper or electronically) and make sure you include the following details:

- Job title
- Company name
- Contact person
- Date résumé sent
- Résumé confirmation (confirmation that they received it)
- First interview
- Thank-you note sent
- Second interview
- Notes/general

Check out www.cv.co.nz/templates for a free MS Excel job progress template.

DRESSING TO WIN

In a recent online poll, 82 percent of respondents agreed with the statement 'Workplace dress codes are slipping'. In the accompanying article, a lawyer at a top-tier firm said young female lawyers wore the same outfit 'on a Monday morning at the office that you see at a club on Saturday night'.

Our dress standards may be slipping, but an interview is the key time to ensure that you are seen as a strong candidate who presents themselves professionally.

It is important to think about what you will wear to the interview three or four days in advance. Make sure everything fits, and give yourself enough time to buy a new shirt, get new shoes or dry-clean your suit if needed.

Wearing a professional outfit may not guarantee you the job, but wearing inappropriate clothes will definitely count you out. As a general rule, think about what the person interviewing you will wear as they go about their day-to-day business and dress one notch up from there. It is far better to be overdressed than underdressed. Being underdressed will destroy your confidence in an interview.

A friend of mine once relayed a story about a young man going into a sail makers for an apprenticeship. As he was neatly dressed in a suit, he received some sniggers from the floor staff who were all dressed in shorts and T-shirts. However, the manager who employed him was also dressed in a suit and offered him the job on the spot. The young man demonstrated he took the opportunity seriously and portrayed himself as a professional who was ready and willing to learn.

If you are not sure about the company's dress code, check with the person who scheduled your interview or contact the HR department and ask. They will be genuinely pleased that you care enough to find out.

Accessories

Do not have too many distracting accessories. For example, large noisy bangles, gaudy necklaces or giant earrings distract from your overall message and what you are trying to communicate in the interview.

Piercings

I once interviewed a candidate who had eight eyebrow rings, for the role of sales representative. I asked if he was prepared to take them out for the interview with a rather conservative client, and his response surprised me: 'I want to sympathize with the pain my wife went through when she had our children,' he said. 'Having them in my eyebrow helps me to feel the pain she went through.' Obviously he did not understand that the pain of childbirth exceeds that of getting an eyebrow pierced! He also placed his sympathy with her pain ahead of providing financially for her and their children. I did not send him to the interview and didn't put him forward for any other roles with the consultancy.

Perfume / Aftershave

Do not over-apply these products. The interviewer does not need to be able to smell you over the far side of the room.

Hairstyle

If you are going for a professional role, always have your hair looking professional and relatively conservative. Unless you are applying for a creative role in advertising or fashion, strange tones and weird looks do not work. Again, they distract from the key message of what you can offer the company.

Tattoos

Hide tattoos as well as you can. If you have them on your forearm, wear a long-sleeved shirt.

Clothing—Women

Do not wear anything low-cut or revealing. Showing large amounts of cleavage or having a high skirt is just cheapening the interview, and the candidate may be perceived to be trying to get the role through their sex appeal. If you have to resort to wearing something sexy to get the job, do you really want to work with the type of people who would employ you?

Makeup should be light and used just to enhance the natural features of your face. Do not cake on foundation or apply bright lipstick.

If you are going for an administrative role, remember that you may need to do some PC-based testing. Therefore, nails should be kept to a minimum length. On one occasion I had to give a candidate a pair of scissors to cut back her brand-new fake nails so that she could complete a typing test the clients had asked for.

Clothing—Men

Please, no wacky ties, they just make you look like a joke. Also, no bow ties. The only professionals that can get away with wearing these are people who have a red nose, wear large shoes and work for a circus. Never wear shorts to an interview. Shorts say, 'I am not really interested in this position'.

WHAT NOT TO BRING TO THE INTERVIEW

Just as important as what not to wear, is what to not bring to an interview. Remember you are being judged *every second* you are being interviewed. Things not to bring (or at least put in your bag before arriving) include:

- An iPod or MP3 player
- Magazines
- Cigarettes
- Gum

- A large, bulky or unprofessional handbag
- A family member or friend hanging out in the reception area (or car park if it is visible).

Transport

Make sure that your mode of transport is suitable for meeting your future employer. Don't turn up to an interview with Greenpeace in a car belching smoke and leaking oil. If necessary, park up the road and walk the last three minutes to the interview. It will also give you some good time to clear your head.

Shoes

Nice shoes are critical to your whole 'look'. Too many times we have interviewed professional-looking people, only to discover that their expensive suit is matched with a pair of battered sneakers.

Mobile phones

ALWAYS turn your mobile phone off during an interview. You are making the interviewer the main priority during the time you are together. If you forget to turn off the phone and it rings, calmly apologize, turn it off and continue as if you have not skipped a beat. *Do not answer it and carry on a conversation.* Yes—this has happened to me on various occasions and every time it leads to an immediate 'no' in progressing to the next stage.

Also ensure your phone home screen is appropriate for the interview. I have been in meetings where people sit opposite me, with their phone displaying attractive people in various states of undress, or swear words in large type size. Not a good look if you are trying to be professional.

Finally if you have an Apple Watch, Samsung Gear, Pebble or similar, make sure your notifications are on vibrate only, or preferably off completely. When your phone or watch starts vibrating, you will not be able to give 100 percent to the interview and it will only disrupt your performance and concentration when you need it most.

Food

Food has no place in an interview (unless you are having an interview at a café or restaurant). Remember if you eat beforehand, to check yourself in the mirror for any food spillages. Also, never ever chew gum during an interview.

Breath

Always have a few breath mints ready in your car or handbag. Interviewing a person with really bad breath is never fun for the interviewer and will dramatically reduce your chances of going through to the next stage.

Trends

It is better to invest in a classic professional suit that will last for a few years, rather than the latest trendy attire that will only last a season.

BODY LANGUAGE

According to many psychologists and experts, body language can account for up to 90 percent of the messages you send during your interview. It is important you portray confidence, and do not take an arrogant or subservient tone.

Posture

Sit up and take genuine confidence from the fact that you have been selected ahead of numerous other candidates for this interview. Sitting up also keeps you alert and on top of your game during this stressful time. Hunching over or sitting on the edge of your chair gives the impression that you are anxious and suffer from low self-esteem. Too relaxed indicates a careless attitude and an underlying arrogance that will be difficult to manage.

Hands and arms

Try not to fiddle with your hands as this can become a major distraction for the interviewer. Ideally, rest your hands on your lap or on the table. Also be aware of clicking pens. I was once reprimanded as a candidate for clicking a pen again and again during an interview.

Try not to cross your arms as this can be seen as a defensive or 'closing off' gesture, shutting the interviewer out.

Eye contact

Eye contact is very important. However, too much is unnerving and not enough portrays a lack of confidence. In some cultures, looking directly at a potential employer is a sign of disrespect. However, this is not true in Western cultures and you will seriously damage your chances if you are looking at the floor all the time.

When you are answering a question, hold brief eye contact for four to eight seconds before looking away briefly; then re-establish eye contact. When listening to a person, establish longer eye contact, but look around every so often so you do not 'stare them out'.

In panel interviews, give the person who asked you the question the most attention, shared with periodic glances to the other interviewers to ensure they feel included.

Voice

No matter how out of control you may feel, try and keep your voice calm and measured. Do not rush answers, and attempt to portray a confidence when you speak. Do not speak in a monotone, but also do not vary your pitch too much.

I remember interviewing a candidate for a customer services role who seemed really good. The interview was progressing well until he started putting on different voices and accents and became overly animated. This started to concern me somewhat and the interview was finished soon after.

HOW TO PREPARE EFFECTIVELY FOR THE INTERVIEW

Find out about the organization. Use resources such as the internet or your local library. Investigate questions such as:

- How many staff do they have?
- What products or services do they sell?
- What is their internal culture?
- What is the 'going rate' of this type of role in the marketplace?
- What do you actually want as a salary? (See 'Successful Salary Negotiation')

That little bit more knowledge you are armed with may be the difference between you getting the job and not getting it.

Review your ability and experience for the job, ensuring you understand all your achievements, skills and experiences, as well as being able to relate this information to the role for which you are applying.

Set three targets to communicate during the meeting. For example:

1. Strong background in sales and account management.
2. Passion for the banking and finance industry.
3. Bachelor of Commerce degree from your University.

It is up to you to ensure the interviewer has as much information as they need about your skills, abilities, experience and achievements to make a decision about taking you through to the next stage—or even employing you on the spot. If you sense there is a misunderstanding about some information, ensure it is clarified before leaving.

Confirm the address and time of the interview a couple of days prior to the interview. Also ask if there is parking or whether you will you have to catch public transport.

Know the main interviewer's name. Not many things are more embarrassing than turning up at a company of 500 staff for an interview and then forgetting the name of the person you are there to see. It makes you look unprofessional and disorganized.

Prepare answers to standard, broad questions about yourself. In about 95 percent of interviews there are some general questions asked, which you can prepare for.

Practice an interview with a colleague, friend or relative. Remember—practice makes perfect.

Dress appropriately for the job: if you are going for a professional sales role, wear a suit; if you are going for a baker's job, wear smart casual. Think of what the employer will be wearing, then 'go one step up' from them. If they wear a polo shirt, wear a business shirt with no tie. You do not want to be underdressed.

Aim to be outside the front door of the building about fifteen minutes prior to your interview. If you are early, go for a walk, clear your mind and then enter the building about five minutes before the scheduled time of your interview.

Never go in half an hour early. Doing this does not say, 'I am keen.' It says, 'My time is more valuable than yours, so hurry up and interview me.'

There is no excuse for being late. No matter what happened (flat tire/ran out of petrol/trapped yourself in a toilet etc.), being late says to the employer you cannot organize yourself and should not be hired!

Get in touch with each of your verbal referees to ensure you have their authorization to use them. Remember to thank them for the time they will be spending speaking to potential employers on your behalf.

Try to take something new to the interview, such as references and examples of work. This way you have more information and you will look highly organized (even if you are not).

Pre-interview stress

If you get 'the butterflies' (that sick feeling in your stomach), do not panic. This feeling is actually a sign that adrenaline is rushing through your body. This means you quickly become more alert to your surroundings. 'Butterflies' are a good sign that you are mentally ready. As long as the butterflies do not 'take over', you will be able to give stronger answers to your potential employer.

The only time things go wrong is when we let the butterflies get the better of us and we start sweating. A great way to relax is to do some quick relaxation exercises such as taking long deep breaths.

When someone says to you 'Don't be nervous' they are being unhelpful. You are presumably going to an interview for a job you want to be successful in getting. You have something to lose and you are exposing yourself to potential rejection from the interviewer. Therefore, it is okay to be a little nervous. You are perfectly normal. However, do not let the butterflies take over.

Ways to relax . . .

It is vital not to show your nerves in an interview. While you may be on edge, it is important to take some time before the interview to calm down and relax as much as possible. The following are some tried and tested ways to calm your nerves just before you step in the door.

- Listen to relaxing music.

- Arrive half an hour early and go for a walk.

- Have a hot thermos of your favorite herbal tea ready to drink before the interview.

- Meditate or pray.

- Take slow deep breaths to improve oxygen flow and slow down your heart rate.

- Phone a family member or friend and have a nice relaxed chat.

- Eat an apple or piece of fruit (not something fizzy that will give you wind).

- Read part of an inspirational magazine, book or blog.

- Do some muscle-stretching exercises.

- Brainstorm your 'bucket list'. A bucket list is a list of all the things you would like to see, do and achieve before you 'kick the bucket'.

- Mentally write a letter to a friend.

The power of visualization

Visualizing a great interview can be very powerful and significantly increase your chances of job success. Psychologist Alan Richardson wanted to understand the effects of visualization on personal performance. In his research study, he selected a number of basketball players and initially measured their free throw percentage success. After this, he randomly assigned the athletes to one of three groups.

Group one went to the gym and practiced making free throws for one hour, five days a week for a month.

Group two also met at the court at the same time, but would be taken through a guided visualization program for one hour. During this time they would picture in their minds picking up a basketball, preparing the free throw and making a successful shot over and over again.

Group three was the control, and they were told not to touch a basketball for one month.

The results:

Group one, who had physically practiced, improved their free throw percentage by 24 percent.

Group two, who had not made a single free throw in 30 days, actually increased their free throw percentage by 23 percent. This was only one percent lower than those who practiced every day for one hour.

Group three stayed stable with their initial performance.

The conclusion:

When you visualize a positive outcome, such as performing excellently in an interview, your mind starts to believe it can be achieved and works toward this goal. Create in your mind the 'finished product', showing your brain what a really successful interview looks and feels like.

Before your next interview, try this technique and see how it works for you:

- Stop and think about the environment. What does the room look like? Who is there? How does the first minute of the interview go?

- From here, start visualizing that the interview is going really well. How does this make you feel? What are some positive results and emotions that are coming out of the interview? What is the feedback you are receiving?

- Finally, think about how the interview ends and the great feeling you get from an interview that went really well.

DURING THE INTERVIEW

When you arrive, open the door to the reception, relax and smile. Introduce yourself to the receptionist and be very polite. People have missed out on jobs because they were rude or abrupt to the receptionist. When you meet the person who will interview you, have a pleasant but firm handshake.

Bring two copies of your résumé to the meeting: one for you to refer to; another to give to the interviewer if they don't have enough copies to go around for all the interviewers. This just makes you look that little bit more efficient and prepared.

The interview itself

Answer each question succinctly with no 'waffle'. Speak for 30 seconds to two minutes for each answer. Always show good manners. Always use proper language and avoid slang. Be enthusiastic and friendly.

Ask questions about the position and the organization. If they have answered your questions without you asking them, say in response to the question 'Do you have any questions?' 'Yes, I did, but you answered them all for me. Thank you.'

Be your authentic self, professional yet real. You do no one any favors by pretending to be someone you are not. Even if you get the job, everyone will see that you do not match their expectations.

Try to understand the question behind the question. In the end, every question comes down to 'Why should I recruit you?' Be sure that you attempt to answer that underlying question completely.

Only about 25 percent of our communication is oral, or what we say. Be aware that your voice inflection, the way you sit, and the way you 'hold yourself' all count toward you getting your dream role.

Display integrity at all times. I once had a young man brag to us in response to our question 'Please give an example of how you think outside of the box?' He was very forthcoming in telling us that he had helped a previous employer illegally overcome a software security program designed to stop the use of software the company had not paid for. If this had not totally turned us off the candidate, he then informed us that he also identified a security flaw in another company's website and exploited it. Not the sort of person we wanted in our team!

If, at the end of the interview, you are excited about the position, tell the interviewer(s) that you are. Make sure they are aware that you want to work for the company and that you are happy with the role as described. Too many people have missed out on positions because they were 'too professional' and gave the impression that they were not interested in the opportunity.

After the interview

Always ensure that you follow up the meeting with an appropriate thank you email. This is another opportunity to sell yourself to the employer and will only improve your chances. An example of such an email is given in the box below.

> Dear [name of person who interviewed you],
>
> Thank you for the opportunity to meet with you yesterday afternoon for the position of [job title].
> [If relevant, add two to three lines relating to specifics you may have talked about: specialist knowledge/practical experience you have that is in line with the position's requirements.]
> I enjoyed discussing this role with you and would like to pursue this opportunity further.
> I look forward to hearing from you in due course.
>
> Kind regards,

Remember to always act with integrity when you write and send the thank you letter. I once was to be interviewed for a senior-level human resources role and had already printed off and stamped the thank-you letter, intending to post it if I liked the job opportunity. Arriving early for the interview, I decided to have a coffee at a nearby café and relax before my meeting. At the café, I had a brainwave when I saw a local postbox. 'Great,' I thought, 'I can post the letter now and not have to worry about doing it later.'

Sadly, I decided to follow this very unwise suggestion from myself and dropped the letter into the box. Literally five seconds passed before my mobile phone rang. Answering it, I was informed by the PA to the manager I was about to be interviewed by, that he was sick and could we please make an alternative time. I then sheepishly told her to inform her boss that he could contact me when he was on the mend. Perhaps unsurprisingly, he never called me back to reschedule. I think it may have been a little thing called 'integrity'.

Debrief yourself after the interview. You may want to ask yourself:

- What could I have done better in that interview?
- What questions have I not heard before?
- Did I answer them well?
- Is there a better way to answer the questions?
- What did I do really well?

If you have not heard from an employer within four to five business days of the interview, follow up with a phone call to find out about the status of your application. Always be pleasant and professional with this enquiry.

COMMON EMPLOYER QUESTIONS AND EXCELLENT ANSWERS

One of Europe's leading career specialists, Daniel Porot, studied candidates in job interviews and found that to be successful, you should try to make your answer last between 20 seconds and two minutes. Anything too short does not give enough information to the interviewer; anything longer just drags the interview on and starts to make you look too long-winded.

Personality

Question: Tell me about yourself.
This question is almost always asked in a variety of ways. You need to prepare a short statement with three to four key points focused on the position you are applying for. Generally, talk only about career matters, unless you have relevant personal experience, achievements or qualifications that will promote you in a positive light. Ideally, you only want to provide a general overview or give context for further discussion.

Question: What are your strengths?
Because you have completed your research on the job as well as the company, you will be able to visualize what the employer is seeking. Phrase your answer in this context and give an example of each strength. For example:

- highly motivated

- driven to succeed

- committed to excellence

- enthusiastic team player

- strong verbal and written skills

- committed to self-development

Question: What are your weaknesses?
Choose an area of weakness prior to the interview. Only state one weakness and say what you are doing in order to overcome it. Overcoming a weakness is actually developing a strength. One thing to remember, however, is to try to make it sound genuine. The old answer 'I work too hard' just makes the interviewer want to dig deeper to get a more honest answer.

It is always fun when I ask this question and get in response, 'I do not have any weaknesses.' No matter how accomplished you are, that's an immediate 'fail' in the interview process.

A résumé I redesigned for a client had the following confession prior to my redrafting:

'Weaknesses: A good wine and the opposite sex.'

Question: Would you see yourself as successful?
Always say 'yes' (no one wants to hire a 'loser'), and briefly detail some of your achievements and the goals you are currently working toward.

Question: What is your single greatest achievement?
This is a great question as it almost always catches people out. Talk about your greatest achievement and have a passion about it. Suitable answers may include raising your children or exceeding challenging sales budgets. Remember, however, that this answer will strongly frame the interviewer's impression of you.

While helping a leading insurer, I asked an older woman this question during an interview. She stared straight through me for a few seconds, then turned to the ceiling with her eyes seeming to cloud over. Turning to me again she said sadly, 'I have never really seen myself as an achiever.' While this broke our hearts, it also said that she had no self-confidence and would not be right for the aggressive telesales role we were interviewing for.

Question: What motivates you?

Explain that of course money is important as it pays for your life outside of work. Then highlight how you enjoy the challenges of your career, working within an exciting team etc. Make it seem that—'Yes, money is important, but I come to work for more than money'.

Career related

Question: Why did you leave your last job?

Here the interviewer wants to understand why you have left (or are looking to leave) and see if there were any issues or problems that you may have had and could bring to their company. Always be positive and do not tear apart your last organization. No employer likes hearing a potential employee talking negatively about their last job. It will only give the signal that you may be trouble. Try to be honest, because most of the time the reason is perfectly legitimate. If you did have trouble with your previous employer, talk about how you wanted to develop your skills further, join a new industry or set a new career challenge. Smile a lot and try to be as genuine as possible.

Question: What background do you have in this industry?

Be specific about the experiences and achievements you have had, and make them relevant to the position you are applying for. Sometimes you may not have specific experience, therefore talk about your passion for the industry if you genuinely have one. (For example, in the marine industry—'I own a boat and am a committee member of the local yacht club.')

Question: What is your career philosophy work ethic?

Provide a short and positive statement that sums up your whole approach. For example, 'It is about getting the job done right, first time.' Once you have stated this, provide an example of how you have implemented this philosophy at work in the past. This approach provides a nice and complete statement that supplies a snapshot of your working approach.

Question: How long would you expect to work here if we employed you?
Do not get specific. However, do not show a predilection to job hopping. An employer respects loyalty, not subservience. Make sure they understand that you respect the opportunity and will work hard for the company.

Question: Have you ever been asked to vacate or move on from a job?
Obviously if you have not, say 'no'. If you have, be truthful and to the point but avoid saying negative things about the management or business involved.

Question: Have you ever been disappointed in your career?
Always be positive and honest. Things do not always go our way in careers. There may have been instances where you did not get a promotion or meet a target. Be positive in the retelling but let the interviewer understand this instance was legitimately disappointing.

Team orientation

Question: How would your team mates describe you?
Highlight a couple of examples where you have assisted your team members and how they responded. Then draw a conclusion from this to state some of your key positive attributes. This provides a solid context, rather than just saying, 'They think I am great.'

Question: Are you a team-orientated person?
Outline a few examples of occasions when you have led and

supported team players in their work or on projects you were involved in. Focus on the positive and highlight key aspects that are important in a well-performing team environment (supportive, proactive, loyal, etc.). Be aware that you must not be boastful, yet need to sell your key aspects.

Question: *What do you find difficult about working with team members?*
Be positive and pleasant, but highlight that working with people who do not keep to a task, or who are arrogant in their approach, does not go well with you. However, make certain that the interviewer is left with the impression that you are a patient and supportive team member.

Business knowledge

Question: *What do you know about our business/organization?*
Always research the business beforehand. *Never* go into an interview without knowing about the firm and their core business. If you can find a particular area of personal interest or expertise, mention this at the interview. It shows you did your homework and will impress the interviewer. The exception to this rule is when you meet a recruiter who is screening for a company. Do not be concerned as everyone else who is applying for the position will not know who the company is either.

Question: *Why do you want to work for our business/ organization?*
This is a vital question. They are attempting to find out your motivation for working for this business in particular. Briefly share your knowledge of their business and comment on how your skills, experience and education would fit well with their company. Talk about the development opportunities the company offers, your interest in the industry or their strong brand/presence in the

marketplace. An employer wants you to be excited about their company and will always hire someone who has a passion for the firm over someone who does not show any interest. Once again, this is why you must do your preparation first. It is hard to be passionate about something you know nothing about.

Question: Why should we employ you?
Highlight how your skills, achievements and experience match what the employer is seeking in the successful team member. Remember to read the job advertisement and/or the position description and respond specifically to those key aspects.

Question: Why do you think you would excel at this job?
Highlight your skills, achievements and experiences in line with the personal attributes in the job advertisement and/or the position description. Give examples of how these aspects are what you are good at and what you enjoy.

Question: What would you look for if you were hiring for this position?
Remember to use the personal attributes from the job advertisement and/or the position description, and slant it slightly toward your skills and experience (without giving the game away).

Question: Tell us about your dream job.
Answer in general terms because anything specific will just pigeon-hole you. Talk about a job that has challenges and where you can work with a great team of people. This shows you are flexible and not looking to leave as soon as this 'miracle job' comes along.

Question: Are you willing to relocate/travel for extended periods if required?

Make sure your wife/husband/partner/family are aligned with you before you answer this. Getting the job based on your promise to travel around the world when your wife is pregnant will only lead to major stress. If you do not have to consider someone else, explain that you enjoy the excitement of new challenges and environments and turn the answer into a real positive.

Professional development

Question: What have you done to develop yourself personally recently?

Mention activities that are directly related to the opportunity. These activities are not just courses you have recently completed but could also include voluntary activities or sitting on local/industry committees or boards.

Question: Where do you want to be in five years?

Respond in behavioral terms. For example, do not say 'In the role of human resources manager' to the human resources manager. Instead, respond in a way that shows you are after a challenge, but does not say 'Get out of my way—here I come.' A good example could be: 'In a position that provides a strong challenge within the human resources environment' (or whatever setting you are applying for).

Business improvement

Question: Have you set up any systems or provided any suggestions that improved business performance?

Ensure you have a couple of great examples that you can promptly highlight, remembering to point out the positive result that came from these initiatives.

Question: What have you learned from mistakes on the job?
Things do not always go to plan. Employers understand this and know that no one is Superman or Superwoman. Provide a real-life example that did not do too much damage to a business, and highlight the key points you learnt from the experience.

Management / Leadership

Question: Describe your management style.
Describe a couple of occasions when you have led staff to achieve a positive result, then detail your style from these examples. Highlight how you managed each situation on a case-by-case basis and judged each situation on its merits.

Question: What would previous managers say about you?
Talk about attributes that are true of you as a person (do not say 'my vibrant personality' if you are a real introvert). Be ready to provide some examples to back up these attributes. Good examples include proactive, loyal, friendly, caring, disciplined, focused and strong leader.

Question: How are you in pressure/stressful situations?
Provide a couple of positive examples of how you were involved in pressure situations, how you coped (remember to be positive, yet real), and what steps you took to resolve them.

Question: What qualities do you look for in a manager/team leader?
Be positive and talk about general traits that you would like in your ideal manager. Try not to make these too constrictive, and do not go on for too long. Positive traits include a sense of humor, fairness, trustworthiness and dependability.

Question: Have you ever helped team members in a dispute?
Detail a positive encounter that you successfully resolved. Talk about the experience and highlight your constructive and high-level problem-solving skills. If this then led to the team members involved having an improved working relationship, mention this too.

QUESTIONS TO ASK AN EMPLOYER

Always prepare questions to ask. Having no questions prepared sends the message that you are only interested in the money and do not care about the company or the job opportunity.

If the employer answers all your prepared questions through the interview without you getting to ask them, just say in response to them 'Yes, I did, but you answered them all for me. Thank you.'

Do not ask questions that are clearly answered on the company's website or in any brochures/material provided by the employer in advance of the interview. This simply says that you did not prepare effectively for the interview and you are wasting the employer's time.

Understand also that you should not spend any longer than 15 to 20 minutes in an interview asking your questions. On one occasion a good friend and I were interviewing a candidate for a senior management role. Realistically, we could both see he was totally unsuitable for the position within the first five minutes of talking with him; however, we felt we would keep going with the interview to give him the benefit of the doubt. After 45 minutes we finished our questions and then asked if he had any. At that stage he pulled out a notebook and proceeded to randomly fire questions at us for about 30 minutes. A lot of the questions were not relevant to the role and it seemed that he had just looked at a few career guidance books and threw the top 40 questions together to impress us. When the onslaught finally finished, he put the notebook down and I breathed a sigh of relief that it was over. Sadly, he then pulled out another journal and proceeded to ask us further non-relevant questions for another 20 minutes. In the end we had to respectfully ask him to shut his notebook and drew the meeting to a close.

Below are some typical questions you could ask an employer. Do not ask too many questions as it may frustrate the interviewer. Just identify the most appropriate ones.

Teamwork

How big is the team I'd be working in?

Who would my co-workers be and what are their functions?

What is the manager's leadership style?

How often would we interact?

What qualities/skills does the manager prize most in their team members?

Team management

How many people would I be managing?

How would you characterize the management philosophy of this organization?

What sort of communication style works best with this team?

How much authority will I have in running the department?

What are the main challenges associated with the team?

Are there any difficult personalities on the staff?

What condition is morale in, and why?

Business strategy

What are the company's objectives for the next 12 months/5 years? What are the significant trends in the industry?

Do you have plans for expansion?

How do you see the future for this industry?

Competitive edge

What makes this company different from its competitors?

What are the company's strengths and weaknesses compared to its competition?

What do you think are the greatest opportunities facing the organization in the near future?

What do you think are the biggest threats facing the organization in the near future?

Corporate culture

What are the company's values?

What can you tell me about the culture and the environment? What do you like about this company? What keeps you here?

What are the traits and skills of people who are the most successful within the organization?

What does the company and team members do for fun?

Personal performance

If I was successful in this role, what would I need to achieve within the first three months?

How do you see me benefiting the company?

If I exceed the company's performance expectations, will there be additional opportunities to expand my responsibilities?

Would there be opportunities for advancement? How long might it be before I am considered for one?

How would you characterize successful employees in this department?

What are their common qualities?

How will my performance be measured? By whom? How often?

Personal development

What does your company do to encourage further education?

What are the opportunities for professional training/further education?

What is the company's policy on providing seminars, workshops and training so employees can keep up their skills or acquire new ones?

How much guidance or assistance is made available to individuals in developing career goals?

Position specifics

Could you explain your organizational structure?

Please describe the duties of the job for me. Can you describe a typical day for someone in this position?

What would you consider to be the most important aspects of this job?

What are the challenges I would face in this position over the next three months?

What will be the greatest challenge in this job overall? What responsibilities have the highest priority?

How much time should be devoted to each area of responsibility? Which customers would I be interacting with most frequently?

What are their typical expectations?

Could you tell me about the way the job has been performed in the past?

What improvements would you like to see happen?

Why is this position vacant? Is this a new position or am I replacing someone?

Why isn't this job being filled from within?

What were the major strengths and weaknesses of the last person who held this job?

What are some examples of the achievements of others who have been in this position?

Where have successful employees previously in this position progressed to within the company?

What types of skills do you not already have on board that you are looking to fill with a new hire?

How do you feel about creativity and individuality in this role?

Are there other job responsibilities not mentioned in the advertisement?

How often will I have to travel in this role?

Department strategy

What is the size of the division, sales volume, earnings? What are the goals of this department?

What have been the division's goals in the last year, and did it meet them?

What have been the department's successes in the last couple of years?

What would be the goals of the department in the coming year? What are the career paths in this department?

How is this department perceived within the organization?

What problems or difficulties are present in the department now?

Salary / Remuneration

What is the salary range?

What are the package benefits—for example, mobile phone, car, health insurance?

Closing

I am very interested in pursuing this job further. What is the next step in the hiring process?

How soon do you expect to make a decision?

What are the next steps in the interview process?

EFFECTIVELY NEGOTIATING YOUR SALARY

SUCCESSFUL SALARY NEGOTIATION

Basic negotiation techniques

You can be highly successful in the salary negotiation process if you stick to some basic techniques of negotiation and have a clear sense of what you are seeking.

Employers expect you to negotiate your salary, so do not let the process be too daunting.

Find out what the position is paying

Before you start the process you must have an understanding of what the role is paying. You can do this in a number of ways:

1. The salary package may be highlighted in the advertisement or in the job description. While the original advertisement online or in the newspaper may not mention total salary, if you dig a little deeper, it may well be covered in-depth within the position description.

2. Analyze similar vacancies on the internet to see what information is available on their remuneration packages.

3. There are a large number of career calculators and databases that provide general analysis of what different types of roles are paying.

4. Contact two or three local recruiters who specialize in your industry and ask for their thoughts on what a role like this would be worth.

If you are still not sure, think about what you are worth to an employer. What have you previously been paid? What are the benefits you are used to? Consider an amount you would be happy receiving if you were successful, then think of a figure you would grudgingly accept. That is now your bottom limit.

Remember that this bottom limit may also drop again for the 'ideal job'. Of course, for your ideal job there are many other benefits aside from money.

Sell yourself effectively

Why are you worth this amount of money? Why will you be an asset to the company? Come up with some concrete and tangible examples and include these during the interview.

It is not just about the money

Whenever you are negotiating your salary, do not forget to take a look at the other benefits, such as company car, mobile phone, retirement plans, medical insurance, holidays and associated advantages. These non-cash factors can make a very average salary package very attractive indeed.

Doing the deal

If an employer asks you, 'How much are you seeking for this position?', immediately turn the tables on them by asking, 'What range do you have in mind?' On some occasions, this will put the employer on the back foot and they will tell you what the company has in mind.

If the interviewer still does not reveal their figure, reply with a broad salary band, rather than a specific value. For example, 'I'm seeking a salary between X and Y.' If you are pressed about the difference in the range, explain that this depends on the other benefits (car, phone, amount of travel).

GENERAL TIPS

- Enter salary negotiations with a solid understanding of your skills, achievements and experience and what they are worth to the employer.

- Try not to be the first to bring up this subject. Make it seem that you are interested in the role, the company and career opportunities first, and money second.

- However, if as the second interview is closing, you are still not sure what the role is paying, find out. You do not want to go to two more interviews and complete a battery of psychological tests to find the salary is much less than you are seeking.

- Ask about further career development and learning opportunities. Job progression is an important aspect in making your salary decision.

- Make certain the person you are talking to actually has some negotiating power. This may not always be the case if you are dealing with a recruiter or HR manager. Generally speaking, the only person who can decide what you finally get paid is your direct manager (as it comes directly out of their budget).

- Salary negotiation is all about psychology and how far you wish to push a point. It does not matter how many books you read, it all comes down to the moment you have to actually sit and negotiate face-to-face with your potential employer.

- If you manage to gain more than you were expecting for your salary, think what it amounts to over three years and try to save it. This could equate to a modest car or an incredible holiday overseas!

- Happiness is more important than salary. Having a shorter commute, more vacation time or good medical benefits might matter more than a small amount more per month.

BEING PROACTIVE

WHAT IF IT ALL GOES WRONG?
HUNTING DOWN OPPORTUNITY

Job-hunting is to some degree like playing the lottery. The more tickets you buy, the increased chance you have of winning a big prize. You have to be in to win! From an employment perspective, the more résumés you have out there representing you in the marketplace, the higher the chance you have of an employer reading it, interviewing you and giving you your dream job. The more potential employers you can inform about your availability, the higher the chance of you becoming employed.

Take a disciplined and professional approach. Make yourself accountable to someone if you tend to procrastinate, like me. This could be a friend, your partner or a family member. You will find that you are far more disciplined and successful if you have someone giving you a 'prod' now and then.

One of the best pieces of advice I ever gained was from a poster I remember seeing when I was about 22 years old. The photo showed an old basketball hoop that had not seen a ball aimed at it in many years. Paint was peeling off the backboard, the wall was water-damaged and spider webs clung to the forlorn and rusty hoop. Underneath was written: **OPPORTUNITY**
Then the words that changed my life:

You miss 100 percent of the shots you do not take.

Immediately, I was hit by the incredible truth of the statement. Successful people do not give up. They just keep going and going until they get the results they want. On most occasions they were not the most intelligent, the loudest or the bravest. 99 percent of the time they were just the most persistent—pressing on when everyone else gave up.

Job-hunting should become a 'nine to five' job too. Early on in the job-hunting process, there is a temptation to 'ease up' when the sun comes out, or go surfing when the waves are just right. However, to take full advantage of your unemployed position, you must treat job-hunting as a full-time role until you are successful in landing a job. If you do not take the process seriously early on, you will find that your financial situation can quickly unravel, and you will wish you had got 'stuck in' a lot earlier.

Tactical job-hunting versus the Shotgun approach

There are two main ways to job-hunt:

1. Approaching companies or recruiters who are advertising available positions that suit your needs and skills (Tactical).

2. Approaching companies that do not seem to be advertising positions that suit your needs and skills (Shotgun).

Applying online via job boards

Online career sites or job boards are great because you can often set up job alerts. You will then be automatically sent an email with positions that match your requirements.

THE 'HIDDEN CAREER MARKET'

The risk is that once you have gone through and applied to the relevant roles on the internet and in the newspaper, you think, 'Well that's it. There are obviously no more positions available today. I will now go to the beach.'

It is estimated that only 25 percent of vacant jobs are advertised on the internet, in classified ads and through employment agencies. This is the most popular way to find work as it is the easiest way to access job openings and you do not have to market yourself too hard. The negative side to this is that all the other job-seekers are also using these ways to find work too, so competition is very intense.

The other 75 percent of available jobs exist in the 'hidden job market'. These vacant positions are 'hidden' because they are filled without employers advertising them on the internet or in newspapers. However, finding these jobs requires a more proactive, focused, disciplined and strategic approach.

You can find out about these 'hidden' job openings by developing strong contacts and networks as well as contacting employers directly via the telephone, email or face to face. When you enter the hidden job market, you may also discover that you are the only candidate who is applying for the job.

Saving the employer money

When we suggest this approach to candidates, they generally say to us, 'Won't the employer be annoyed and think I am wasting their time?' On the rare occasion this may be true; however, most employers welcome this direct approach for a number of reasons:

- *Recruitment fees*. The average recruiter charges between 12 and 15 percent of a person's salary to place the candidate. The employer will end up paying an amount top of your salary for the privilege of hiring you. Therefore if you approach them directly it *immediately* saves them thousands. This becomes very important for a small-to-medium sized enterprise that does not have the same cash reserves as a larger employer.

- *Immediate solution*. If a person hands in their notice, the employer only has a very short period of time to find their replacement. If that person is not found quickly, it can become a major issue for the employer, with all the other members of the team having to 'pitch in' just to get by. Therefore, if you can start straight away, make that apparent to the employer as this may well be the difference between gaining the role and not.

- *Saving the employer time.* A manager is employed to do a particular job. However, when someone leaves, that employer now has to do their current role, plus spend an extra five to 15 hours a week trying to recruit the new team member. If they pick you instead, they will save themselves hours of unproductive business time and they can be getting on with the job they are actually paid for.

- *Proactivity and passion.* By going direct to an employer, you are demonstrating the exact skills they would wish to have in an employee. As well as this, you are honoring them by effectively saying, 'I could have chosen anywhere where I wanted to work, but I chose you.' As an employer myself, it is always a nice feeling when someone thinks my company would be a great place to work.

- *No hassle.* On many occasions the employer would be happy to recruit a person who has an eight out of ten skill rating and who lives nearby, rather than search for a nine out of ten candidate who may end up living on the far side of town. If you live near the employer, make this very clear as they can then be assured you can always start on time and will not be held up by traffic jams and bad weather.

GET PROACTIVE AND KNOCK ON DOORS

As mentioned, many employment statistics state that no more than 25 percent of all vacancies are ever advertised. This leaves the field wide open for those who are prepared to do a little more than scan jobs websites or read the vacancies section of newspapers.

Make a list of key companies you would like to work for and approach them directly. Or take your pick of the top firms in your field of interest and contact them.

This approach to job-hunting is called 'cold calling' and it puts candidates in the driving seat. You scan the employment market—rather than the job market—and directly approach firms you want to work for. This takes initiative and determination, but it is often worth the effort.

A young family friend decided to use this method recently, and visited a top five-star lodge to drop off her résumé. She was looking for any type of work and was just hoping to get a starting role so she could develop her hospitality skills further. Immediately the manager was impressed with her 'go to it' style and offered her a permanent position six days a week, five hours a day in housekeeping. Her new employer is now only five minutes down the road and the job lets her have a wonderful lifestyle.

Finally, do not be afraid to offend some people during this process. It is more important that you find a great job and annoy the odd person with a telephone call or email, than apply with everyone else to only the advertised jobs. What's the worst that can happen? The HR manager is not going to drive to your house and throw a brick through your window!

As you will appreciate, I suggest that you take both approaches in your job search (Tactical and Shotgun). As stated, it is all about the number of résumés you can get out into the marketplace.

The power of the 'elevator pitch'

Have a 10-second 'elevator pitch' always prepared, covering three to four key points you want to highlight to the employer. The term 'elevator pitch' was developed in the heady days of the 'dotcom' boom in the late nineties. It was a term start-up companies came up with to communicate to a venture capitalist their business, its key offerings and financial returns in less than 30 seconds—the time it takes to get in and ride an elevator up ten floors.

The key here is to use short and powerful statements that meet the needs of the employer. For example, if you were a customer services officer, you would want to potentially highlight the following key points:

- Genuine passion for helping people.
- Five years' experience as a customer services officer.
- Recently completed a diploma in business.

If you wanted the role of operations manager in the transport industry, the points may be:

- Twelve years' experience in freight forwarding and logistics.
- Excellent knowledge of importing and exporting regulations.
- Strong and trusted network within the domestic transport industry.

Have this elevator pitch always ready in your mind, as the next telephone call you answer may well be a recruiter wanting to pick your brain and find out if you are suitable for their available position.

THE INFORMATIONAL INTERVIEW

Dick Bolles, author of the best-selling career guide *What Color Is Your Parachute?*, highlights a great way to get in the door of a company or industry you are interested in working for. This technique is called the 'informational interview'.

The informational interview is designed to gain information about a job, career path, industry or company. While it is not a job interview, you are sitting in front of a key decision-maker in the company and building strong networks that you can hopefully leverage later on.

Do your research on an internet site such as LinkedIn and find the name of a key person within the department in which you are interested. Contact them directly and say, 'I am interested in developing a career in sales (or whatever your field of interest is) and would like to meet with you to find out about your company and industry.'

Do not worry about disturbing them, as on many occasions they will feel flattered that you decided to contact them directly. In my 20 years in the recruitment and human resources industry, I only had one person ask to come in for an informational interview and of course I said 'yes'.

Important: Do not suddenly change the tone of the interview from informational to job-seeking. The second you begin trying to pitch yourself, the employer will feel misled and will quickly terminate the interview.

I was once approached by a woman having no luck returning to the workforce after raising two children. She had gone down all the usual channels of applying for advertised jobs via job boards and newspapers, but as she had not been working for five years, she kept running and losing against candidates who had recent work experience. After applying for 100+ jobs and not receiving a single interview, her spirit was broken and her self-esteem was at an all-time low.

We firstly helped her define her achievements so she could explain these to an employer in a succinct way. We then helped her understand about the 'hidden job market' and how a direct approach to employers could benefit her. Now all excited about her achievements and what she could offer a company, she then visited a range of small-to-medium-sized local employers with her résumé.

After only half a day, she had secured a formal job interview which in turn led to a job offer later that week. One of the main reasons why the company chose her was that she was family focused and that fitted in completely with their organization's ethos.

NETWORKING

Use your own personal and business networks to spread the word. Surprisingly, most people in your city know each other through probably only two to four degrees of separation. Therefore, ensure your networks know that you are seeking a new position.

People trust their friends, so if you are referred to an employer by a friend, you come with a higher level of trust than others who just come in off the street.

Time and time again we find people who have gained employment by just telling their friends and family that they are seeking work. On many occasions a company may have a new position that has just come up or a person that has just handed in their resignation. If people in your network know your skills and abilities, they are in a prime place to mention you to their employer or contact you to get your résumé ready for action.

Networks include:

- LinkedIn
- Clubs
- Toastmasters
- Facebook
- Sports clubs
- Schools
- Church
- Rotary
- Local employers
- Local pub

What networks could you utilize today to spread the word?

BEING PROFESSIONAL ON- AND OFFLINE: YOUR 'ONLINE TATTOO'

As mentioned earlier, employer surveys show that up to 93 percent of recruiters actively use social media as a key screening tool.

Everything you do leaves a mark online and either positively or negatively affects your personal brand. Every post, comment, tweet and picture leaves a social history of you that becomes your 'online tattoo'.

One second from disaster

While social media can be incredibly useful to promote and market your brand effectively, it is the ultimate double-edged sword.

To develop a strong and trusted brand takes years, positioning yourself with key influencers and wisely creating content that adds values in peoples lives. However, all this good work can be undone in a second by one poor choice.

Why do employers disregard candidates after screening online?

Job-seekers must understand that the information they post online is readily accessible to not just their friends and family, but also their potential employers. A CareerBuilder UK survey found that 53 percent of employers reported they discovered content on social networking sites that caused them not to employ the candidate. The main reasons for not recruiting a candidate included:

- Lying about their courses/qualifications—38 percent

- Poor communication skills—31 percent

- Racist/discriminatory comments—13 percent

- Information about drinking or using drugs—10 percent

- Provocative or unsuitable photographs or text—9 percent

- Putting down previous employers,
  colleagues or clients—9 percent
- Sharing private/confidential information—8 percent.

As a recruitment and HR professional, I find it amazing what people will put online and share with the world at large. I have viewed photos of people almost nude, read racist comments and am always coming across swearing/foul language of some kind. It is vital that anyone looking to be employed does an assessment of their 'online self', taking down any 'dodgy information' that may be negatively perceived by an employer. What used to be behind closed doors is now wide out in the open.

However, the same study showed that you can increase your chances of a successful application through the correct use of online media. 50 percent of the employers questioned said they found content on the candidate's social networking site that caused them to think favorably about the person. Top examples include:

- Their profile lined up with their qualifications—61 percent
- Demonstrated strong/solid communication
  skills—41 percent
- Candidate came across as being well-rounded—37 percent
- The profile provided a good feel for the candidate's
  personality and their 'fit' in the company—28 percent
- Candidate appeared to be creative—24 percent
- Provided a professional appearance/image—22 percent
- Received awards and accolades—15 percent
- Others posting good references about
  the person—15 percent

SOCIAL MEDIA DISASTERS

Facebook

A great example of how powerful a role social media can play in your career is provided by the case of Kyle Doyle, a 21-year-old resolutions expert for telecommunications firm AAPT, who got into trouble with his employer for taking a sick day off work. Unfortunately for him, he posted the following Facebook status update: 'I am not going to work. F#@& it I'm still trashed. SICKIE WOO.' Sadly, he forgot that his immediate boss was a friend on Facebook and therefore quickly became aware of his situation.

Further fallout from this story will occur when any new employer looks up Kyle online. If he has open Facebook settings selected for his account, his online life will be visible and he will appear to be a poor candidate who is happy to lie to his employer.

Remember that it is not just your own content people can have access to. Friends on Facebook may have compromising photos or content relating to you on their site, so remember to visit these and ask your friends to remove any that may be perceived as negative. If there is a picture of you smoking on Facebook, but your résumé states you are a non-smoker, it can seriously undermine your integrity.

Selfies

In March 2015 Christina Freundlich, a former Political Communications Professional for the Iowa Democratic Party, made the ultimate social media mistake by posting an Instagram selfie of herself smiling beside the site of a New York gas explosion that killed two people.

International media retribution was swift, with her unwise decision not only impacting her future career, but also hurting her former employer. As well as this, her brand is now forever tarnished as hundreds of newspapers and media outlets around the world reported the story.

Twitter

PR executive Justine Sacco should have known better when she posted a racist tweet just before she boarded a flight to Cape Town, South Africa.

The post was retweeted over 3,000 times and was picked up by media outlets around the world, all while Sacco sat unaware during her journey. The hashtag '#hasjustinelandedyet' was trending on Twitter around the world as thousands awaited Sacco's response. Once safely landed, Sacco found out she was also was fired by her employer IAC, who condemned her behavior as 'outrageous' and confirmed to international media that they had 'parted ways with the employee in question'.

Warning!

Do not use Twitter if you are angry or drunk. Quick comments made in a second have a habit of staying around.

Ensuring a positive digital footprint

There are ways, however, to use social media and the internet to your advantage. If you are a business professional, populate your LinkedIn profile with up-to-date information and start making positive contacts with other business professionals and groups online.

Ensure all online material is constructive and positive (both personal and professional) and that it reflects you as a 'whole' person.

Start writing blogs about your area of choice using sites such as Wordpress and Blogger. You will soon be seen as an expert in your area and most importantly Google will slowly build up a profile of you as a leader in your field.

ONLINE PROFILE CHECKLIST

Use the following checklist to assess your online recruitment 'footprint'.

- What websites do you have content on? (Facebook /Twitter/ LinkedIn). What sites do you have content on that you may not have put up yourself (sites belonging to friends/family)?

- What is your profile saying about you? Many times these profiles include information about your favorite films, books and TV shows, religious and political beliefs, your studies and your interests. A good idea is to get someone else to scrutinize your profile and give you their honest feedback, no matter how hard it is to hear.

- Are there any photos that could be taken out of context if an employer viewed them? Photos with alcohol and cigarettes are generally viewed negatively by employers.

- Are you able to improve security/privacy settings so only 'friends'/people you have invited can view your information?

- Are there any negative comments or gripes you may need to delete?

- Are your tweets positive or informative in nature or do they paint a poor picture of you?

- Who are you following on Twitter/friends with on Facebook? What does this say about you?

- Do not talk about your job search online if you are still working for a company.

- Check YouTube for any video content you may unwittingly be a part of.

- Do a Google search on your name and read the first ten or so pages. Anything negative that comes up, try to resolve immediately.

- Work on maintaining a professional profile and update it regularly.

- Is any of your information online confidential in nature? If so, make sure it is deleted or hidden from the casual viewer.

Check your personal voicemail message and your email address

A poor email address can destroy any chance you may have with employment. Anything sexual, too personality driven, or just stupid is a liability. Classic examples I have seen from job candidates include:

- missrandom@xxx.com

- onenightstand@xxx.com

- fcukimdislexic@xxx.com

- shut-tha-far-cup@xxx.com

- justamess@xxx.com

- boididdathurtmyface@xxx.com

- depressedangel@xxx.com

- cruel2dabone@xxx.com

- lifeisanightmare@xxx.com

- dopeyman@xxx.com

If you want to have a fun address, make sure you also set up a work-only email account which you can check periodically during your job hunt.

My favorite story about the dangers of poor email addresses came from a job candidate in the UK. Applying for a range of roles in Wales, he was surprised to find his résumé was getting him nowhere. It was only when a large corporate replied to inform him that he had missed out on another job opportunity did the truth dawn on him. The company's reply stated: 'Thank you for your application. We received a large volume of very high-standard submissions and regret to inform you that you were unsuccessful on this occasion.' The email then went on to say: 'For your future reference, the chances of getting employed in Wales with the email address 'gladimnotwelsh@xxx.com' are virtually nil.'

Your mobile/home voicemail can also be poor quality. Check this to ensure it is also professional.

Do not record voicemail messages like one I heard on a client's phone recently: 'Yo, this is Steve, you know what to do . . . [beep].' Also, if you are applying for a job remember to leave your standard message in the language of the country in which you are applying for jobs in. It is really off-putting for an employer to phone a candidate and then get a voicemail they do not understand. The only time they will know when to talk is when the message beeps. By this stage they would have probably hung up.

Again, this is a major point of contact for an employer so make sure it is professional.

DAMAGE CONTROL

How do you deal with the fact that you were fired from a former position when pitching yourself to a prospective employer? How do you explain a gap of some nature in your career trajectory? We are not perfect candidates after all.

If your total approach is not professional and there are some gaps or issues floating about in your career history, a sharp-eyed recruiter or HR manager should be able to sniff them out. However, as mentioned earlier, your role is to sell yourself and what you can offer an employer—not to give a list of reasons why the employer should not employ you.

Imagine if Ferrari created a supercar called the 'F70'. This new and exciting vehicle will revolutionize premium-level travel and will be the epitome of class and styling. Now imagine if Ferrari has the F70 crash-tested at both the Italian and German safety associations, with the Italian group responding with 3 out of 5 stars for safety and the German organization replying with 5 out of 5 stars for safety. What would the marketing team have on the F70's brochure? They would have 'Crash-tested to German vehicle standards—5 out of 5 stars.' They are not lying, but are being economical with the truth.

In the same way, we must accentuate our positives and try not to go too near discussion of any negative aspects of our career which may stand out.

COMMON ISSUES

Gaps in your career history

A typical situation for many people is time missing in their employment history. Not many people have a perfect work history, moving from one job to another straight away. Because the role of your résumé is to sell you, you want to ensure nothing negative appears to turn the employer off you. Therefore, an option is to only detail the years employed in your résumé and not the months.

For example:

Aug 2012–Current	123 Company
	Customer Services Consultant
Jun 2009–March 2012	ABC Company
	Customer Services Consultant

This highlights immediately to an employer that this person was unemployed for a period of up to five months. This will raise questions in their mind and may become an excuse not to employ them. A way to solve this is to frame the information like this:

2012–Current	123 Company
	Customer Services Consultant
2009–2012	ABC Company
	Customer Services Consultant

Employers will still wish to check these dates; however, they are now in direct contact with you and this can give you the chance to impress them with your great communication skills.

A friend of mine is a very senior executive and was struggling to find employment because he had a large gap in his résumé from his last employment. We asked him what he had been doing since then and he answered that he had done a bit of consulting, some software development and some business planning while trying to find full-time work. We then 'repaired' the missing portion of his résumé to say that he had been self-employed consulting to a range of businesses and had been instrumental in the development of a new HR software program. Suddenly employers saw him as a go-ahead individual with recent work experience. This did the trick and he was employed in a general management role three weeks later.

Took time out to raise a family?

Missing dates can also be perceived as an issue for many 'stay-at-home' mums returning to the workforce. Sadly, even in this day and age, a small amount of employers see raising a family as a very 'basic' activity that adds no value to the employment world. A great way to turn around this negativity is to highlight the time spent raising your children as an opportunity to develop new skills. You can list the key jobs of a stay at home parent as follows:

- Housekeeper
- Cook
- Daycare Centre Teacher
- Facilities Manager
- Computer Operator
- Driver
- Psychologist
- Janitor
- Laundry Machine Operator
- Chief Executive Officer
- Nurse
- Event Planner
- Nutritionist

- Logistics Analyst

- Interior Designer

- Book-keeper

- Administrative Assistant

- Plumber

- General Maintenance Worker

- Groundskeeper

The group determined that a stay-at-home parent should be paid as much as managers in big businesses for their contributions. The stay-at-home parents surveyed said they logged a total of 92 hours a week performing the jobs above.

Following on from this, we once saw a résumé that had the following:

Jun 2010–Mar 2014 **Raising a family**
Key skills gained:
- High level of attention to detail
- Multitasking
- Event management
- Communication / Negotiation
- Budgeting
- Working independently
- Analytical / Problem-solving
- Working to deadlines
- Stress management

This ensured the reader understood that this period of time the candidate was talking about was actively spent sharpening her career skills, not just changing nappies . . . Always remember that an employer who sees no value in this part of your career is not an employer you want to work for. Therefore, if you miss out on a job opportunity because of this reason, it is actually very positive.

It has been a while since you worked

For some of us, time away from our careers could not be helped. This may result from a wide range of reasons, including sickness or death of a loved one, your own ill health or even time taken to spend your lottery winnings. For any of these reasons, and many more, you probably do not wish to have your most recent career history in your résumé, if it finished four years ago. A way around this is to only include the time period you were employed in each of your roles.

For example, if you worked between 2009 and 2012 for 123 Company, and then were employed by ABC Company between 2003 and 2007, the first question that will go through a recruiter's mind will be 'What were you doing for the two years between jobs and what have you been doing since 2012?' If the other candidates have a more complete work history, chances are the recruiter will not even interview you because they see you as not having up-to-date experience.

However, if you phrase the information in the following way, a recruiter will hopefully have enough interest to at least contact you to discuss the time period. In the best-case scenario, they will interview you if the rest of your skills and qualifications match the role.

Four years	123 Company
	Customer Services Consultant
Three years	ABC Company
	Customer Services Consultant

While this is not ideal practice, when the recruiter contacts you, you can then use your charm and communication skills to convince them that you are a viable contender for the role.

Bad / Tricky references

Sometimes things just do not go to plan. Your old manager may not have liked you, may have been jealous of you, or just not liked the school you went to. Sadly, to use them as a referee will only shoot down your chances to be gainfully employed in the future.

This actually happened to me on one occasion. A recruitment friend of mine contacted two of my more recent referees. One was excellent; however, the second was not overly positive. I was shocked at how this could happen, but had to get immediately into damage control mode. Because I had previously been the owner of a recruitment consultancy, I did not have another direct employer to act as a referee. I thought long and hard and came up with a number of alternative verbal referees including:

- Previous business clients at my recruitment consultancy.
- Other 'dotted-line' managers at the insurance company I had a positive relationship with (see below).
- People of note in the industry that I had developed relationships with.
- Respected individuals in the community (for example, justices of the peace and pastors).

This worked very well and I quickly had a number of trusted colleagues I could call upon.

Using 'dotted-line' managers (a manager who you did not report directly to, but still had a day-to-day or week-to-week working relationship with) also works very well. You can still use your most recent company while not running the risk of getting a bad reference from your old boss.

Self-employed

A common complaint from self-employed people is they have no verbal referees they can use. The last time they were employed may have been 30 years ago and their former employers will have moved on or even have passed away.

A recruiter completes verbal references because they wish to examine a wide range of issues such as your work ethic, honesty, ability to reach targets etc. You should therefore ask a few current customers if they will provide a positive recommendation for you. Typical with many small-to-medium employers, the company/client relationship can be very close, with many clients also becoming close friends. Leverage this relationship if you can to help you to get referees who will make you stand out.

Be careful about this, though, as you may not want many of your current customers to know you are about to shut down or sell the company and find other employment.

Other people to contact who can speak about your professionalism and work ethic include your accountant and bank manager.

Remember it is not your job to shoot yourself in the foot, so talk around tricky subjects if possible. If there are difficult questions you think may come up during the interview process, have answers prepared for them in advance.

Remember, at the end of the day, you have to be honest and not lie to any potential employer. Any lies are sure to catch up with you one day.

GETTING PAST THE FEAR BARRIER

In many ways the hardest part of getting your résumé out into the marketplace is getting past the fear barrier of contacting people you do not know. However, remember that you are a *solution to the employer's problem*, therefore they have to hear about you.

In most cases you are either a 'profit opportunity' or a 'cost benefit' to a company. Thinking of yourself in these terms will increase your confidence. Remember, if an employer receives your information and contacts you wanting to find out more, they see the value you can bring to their company and you are now in an exciting and positive position to sell yourself.

What if it all goes wrong?

Not having a job can massively affect your identity and who you see yourself as. If asked 'Who are you?' What is your answer?

The job-hunting period can be incredibly stressful and worrying. Try to be calm about your approach and focus on getting résumés out into the marketplace.

Remember that job-hunting is a numbers game. The more résumés you have in the marketplace, the higher the chance you have of landing your dream role.

Dealing with the pain of negative self-esteem

If you are really running into major self-esteem issues, remember that you have strong values and you deserve a chance. Take active steps to:

- Stop comparing yourself to other people.

- Stop putting yourself down.

- Use affirmations to raise your self-esteem (the opposite of above).

- Mix with positive and supportive people.

- Acknowledge your positive qualities and skills.

- Involve yourself in work and activities that you love.

Areas of support and people you can turn to

Hopefully your family will be the place you can turn to for understanding. Be honest and open with how you are feeling.

Never be afraid to ask for help from anyone. Good areas of support include friends, a local church or clubs you belong to.

In his bestseller *What Color Is Your Parachute?*, Dick Bolles highlights the importance of having four key 'Support Staff'.

- A listener—for when you are feeling down.
- A wise one—for when you are puzzled about what to do next.
- A taskmaster—for when you are lacking discipline.
- A cheerleader—for when you want to share your successes.

However, professional services may also be required if things are really difficult.

Understand that everyone who has ever job-hunted has been plagued by doubt and self-esteem issues while doing it, no matter how successful they seem today.

'OLDSCHOOL'—BUILDING YOUR NETWORK

It's funny that as it is becoming more efficient to communicate with others via Facebook, Skype, email and Twitter, more 'old school' virtues of direct contact are starting to make somewhat of a comeback, especially in terms of personal branding.

Everything you do (both in the virtual and real worlds) either promotes or undermines your brand. Small things like paying an account on time or giving a high standard of service to a customer can also spread via word of mouth, opening up opportunities that would otherwise be closed to you.

A good example of this is a person I know who travels the world as a bartender on cruise ships. He initially got his dream job because of the high standard of customer service he delivered to a client one evening. The person he was serving turned out to be the head of recruitment for a leading cruise line and offered him a job on the spot!

SAYING GOODBYE—YOUR RESIGNATION LETTER

Resignation letters are one of the more difficult types of letters to write. It would be easy to write: 'I QUIT. See you later.' However, most companies require a notice period to be given, and some studies have shown that many employers remember more about your performance during this period than at any other time.

A well-worded letter can help make these last few weeks comfortable, if not enjoyable for everyone; it can help get you a favorable written reference; and it will help the employer to remember you well in the future if a verbal reference is required.

Never burn your bridges—you'll never know when you need to cross them again.

Rules for a resignation letter

- Do not make any negative statements about the business or people or offer ways for the company to 'improve' (in your opinion).

- Clearly state the date you intend to finish and make sure it is the length of time required in your employment contract. Allow extra time if you are able.

- Give a reason why you are leaving; however, you do not need to be too specific.

- Offer to be available to help after you finish. Indicate how the employer can contact you after you have gone, for those 'where did you put the blue folder' type questions.

- Let them know the positive points of your time with them. For example, 'great people', 'provided a valuable stepping stone in your career'.

- No matter how negative, worn out or just keen to move on you are, try to make the letter sound sincere, not sarcastic. These are people who know you and will most likely have noticed any decline in motivation and enthusiasm toward the company/your job.

- Check your spelling and grammar.

- Put the letter in a sealed envelope addressed to your manager, human resources manager or appropriate member of staff.

- Give it to them directly. Do not leave it in a 'pigeon-hole' or on their desk as it may be overlooked or fall into the wrong hands. Then when you come to leave there may be complications as no one will know anything about it.

- Remain professional.

Resignation letter structure

The basic structure of the letter should include four to five paragraphs. Avoid the temptation to be negative or sarcastic in the letter as all this does is undermine your professionalism and the quality work you have provided during your time with the company.

Paragraph one

This should include the reason for your letter—that you want to notify them of your intention to resign from your position and the date you would like to leave on.

To ensure that there are no misunderstandings, include your job title and write the date out in full. This is particularly important if it is a large company and your letter is addressed to the HR manager and not your direct manager.

Paragraph two

This paragraph should explain why you want to leave the company. You do not need to be too specific; however, you want to leave your manager and colleagues feeling comfortable about having you around as you work out your notice.

Examples include:

- I have been offered an opportunity that was too good to refuse and is in line with where I want to take my career long-term.

- I have decided to attend university full-time to obtain a qualification that would benefit my career long-term.

Paragraph three

In this paragraph you have to put in the feel-good factor that will help make life comfortable for everyone while you remain with the company.

This is where you let your employers know of the positive things about the company and the positive impact it has had on you and your career. Compliment your manager on things they have contributed and let them know how valuable the experience has been.

Do not go overboard and do not be insincere—it will be noticed.

Paragraph four

In this paragraph let them know that you are prepared to assist with the smooth transition of work to a replacement employee. Offer to help with training and let them know you are available to answer any relevant questions they may have after you have departed. (Include your mobile phone number and private email address at the bottom of the letter.)

Paragraph five

Thank them once again for everything they have done for you and wish them and the company all the best for the future.

Sign off 'Kind regards' with your name and contact details.

Check out www.cv.co.nz/templates for a free MS Word resignation letter template.

LONG-TERM CAREER PLANNING

Unfortunately, most people think goal setting and career planning is something only people who own Ferraris do. Sadly, the vast majority of people spend far more time planning their wedding or buying a second-hand car than they do planning their life and their career.

As motivational speaker John Eric Jacobsen states:

> 'Your goals are your blueprints for the future. Goals are dreams about to be born. Goals are the ladders we climb to reach our vision of success. If you don't have goals, you end up working for someone who does have goals.'

This is why less than one in 30 people invests in motivational books and programs and actively plans their life through formal goal setting. On a positive note, you are probably one of these people as you are reading these words right now.

When it all goes wrong

As a recruiter, it has always made me sad to see someone like a 45-year-old accountant with two children in exclusive schools, a house in the nicest part of town and two cars hate what their life has become. The typical story was that one of their parents had been an accountant and it seemed a safe bet for a successful career.

What their parents did not factor in when encouraging them to follow in their footsteps was that they hated finance, money and numbers, and actually wanted to be an architect. 20 years later they now wish to change their career, but can't afford to drop their salary to go back to study. They are now trapped in a job they cannot stand and living a lifestyle that can only be paid for by staying in their current career. They are caught in the 'revolving door of affluence' and have become 'rat race refugees' as my good friend and professional speaker Rachel Prosser aptly describes it.

Sadly, they think because they cannot escape from their career, they only need a better-paying position at a better company to balance their life and family out. This almost never works and the person is trapped in an even more senior role that demands more time at the office, more time on the road and less time at the place that matters most—home.

Plan your career

As mentioned at the start of this guide, it is vital you have a clear idea of what both your short- and long- term career goals are. Once you know where you want to head, you can then reverse engineer your path and put in place the small steps required to get there! If you clearly understand your long-term goals, your short-term choices and decisions will be easier to make.

Questions you want to ask yourself include:

- Where do I ultimately want to be in my life, both professionally and personally? Is climbing the corporate ladder important to me, or am I happy with a less stressful (and less well-paid) job?

- What are my strengths and what do I do well? To answer this, ask 10 family members and friends to give you honest feedback.

- What are my weaknesses and what sort of things do I struggle with? Again, ask your family and friends for their honest thoughts.

- What would be a great career choice to make now if I could walk into any role?

- What role do I want to be sitting in within the next 10 years?

- What role do I want to be sitting in within the next 20 years?

- What are 100 things I want to do / have / achieve before I 'kick the bucket'? (i.e. your bucket list)

- What further training or qualifications do I need to attain?
- Can I do these part-time while I am employed?
- What are three things I can do this week to start to achieve both my short- and long-term goals?
- What is my next step?

FINAL THOUGHTS

The job-hunting process can be crushingly hard sometimes. But our team is always there to lend a hand. Visit us at the following addresses:

CV and Career Development

www.cv.co.nz

Goal coaching and professional speaking

www.tomoneil.com

Outplacement

www.outplacement.co.nz

APPENDIX

Lisa Smith is a professional HR practitioner and manager at www.
cv.co.nz. She created this excellent document which opens many
eyes to the hard work mothers put into their day.

Job Description
HOME EXECUTIVE (Both working and non-working)

Position summary
This role is responsible for:
- Running and managing the day-to-day operations of the
  enterprise.
- Ensuring the financial viability of the enterprise.
- Overseeing the physical, mental and emotional
  development and needs of the younger (and therefore
  immature and demanding) team members.
- Perfectly supporting and coordinating the physical,
  emotional and environmental needs of the older colleagues
  in the team.

General responsibilities
- Manage physical needs including feeding, toileting,
  bathing and ensure appropriate exercise and
  developmental activities for younger team members.
- Primarily responsible for all aspects of health and safety.
- Maintain stimulation necessary for age-appropriate
  developmental activities. Offer activities and
  opportunities for creative play and ensure certain
  milestones are achieved, taking every opportunity for
  teaching basic numerical and linguistic, as well as social
  and behavioral, skills.

- Manage the enterprise's emotional (both individual and corporate) needs and requirements. Balance team members' desire for independence and space with reassurance and support. An underlying understanding for the need of discipline and character building is pivotal for this role.
- Be proactive in making and keeping health appointments, social engagements, developmental activities (playgroup and, later, kindy and swimming, etc.) for the younger team members.
- In keeping with social traditions, ensure younger team members are always dressed well and appropriately for the occasion and weather.
- Act as key decision-maker for scheduling, clothing, diet and interior décor.
- Ensure all needs are met immediately if not in advance and doing so with loving support and perfect composure in times of stress and frustration. Perfect wisdom in terms of appropriate responses to every situation is a must.

Day-to-day duties include
- Maintain a clean, healthy, attractive, stimulating and warm environment to a high standard.
- Prepare as many as six meals a day as well as snacks.
- Ensure laundry is cleaned, dried (even in the rain), folded and put away.
- Maintain a clean kitchen (including dishes, microwave, fridge and cabinetry).
- Maintain clean and organized living areas (including dusting, cleaning floors, and general tidying); outside areas to be kept tidy, even after rain, snow and hail.
- Attractive outdoor additions such as trees and vegetable gardens to be developed as well as maintained with water and weeding.

- Driving younger team members to various outside activities including doctor's appointments, shopping,friends, etc.
- Maintain personal emotional and physical health.
- Be attractive and interesting at all times for your partner.

Qualifications

- At least diploma level qualified in psychology, finance, English, mathematics, geography, logistics, beauty, education, hospitality, mechanical engineering, nursing and IT. (Bachelor's level qualifications preferred. Trade certificate in hairdressing is useful for the first three years of each team member's existence.)

Pay

- Between the ages of 10 and 18 you pay them.
- When you die, you give them whatever is left.

Benefits

- Hopefully almost unlimited opportunities for personal growth and free cuddles for life.

ABOUT THE AUTHOR

Tom O'Neil—Bachelor of Social Science (major in Psychology), MNSANZ, MCDANZ

Award winning speaker and bestselling international author Tom is a key contributor on interview preparation and career achievement to numerous international career guides and is a professional speaker on the subjects of personal development and goal achievement. He has been quoted in *What Color is Your Parachute?* every year since 2008, and his work has been translated into more than 10 languages. He has been interviewed on many occasions for various international television and radio shows and has had numerous articles relating to interviewing, goal setting and career development printed in a wide range of magazines and newspapers, including the *Harvard Business Review* and the *Economist*.

After founding and selling two recruitment consultancies, Tom consulted independently in human resources to a number of leading organizations. After two short periods doing community support work through his church in the Philippines and India, he joined Deloitte as a management consultant specializing in human resources.

Tom now owns a number of international career development and professional speaking companies including:

www.tomoneil.com

www.cv.co.nz

www.resumeone.com.au

www.outplacement.co.nz

www.outplacementservice.com.au

As Founder and Managing Director of cv.co.nz, a leading international career consultancy, Tom's systems have been used to create career solutions for more than 10,000 clients from more than 50 countries.

Contact Tom to speak at your event or conference

info@cv.co.nz
twitter.com/tomoneil_com
linkedin.com/in/tomoneil1

If you think we have omitted information, or you would like to suggest new material for addition to this job-hunting guide, please email us at editor@tomoneil.com with your comments.

ACKNOWLEDGEMENTS

Thanks to Laura Rusnak, MPH, CHES, Faculty at University of South Florida for her contribution to the section describing employment experience.

Thank you to my ever patient, loyal and loving wife Sarah (also a writer) and my two boys Tim and Joey who bring so much joy to my life.

Massive thank you to international career expert Gaynor O'Neil, my mom, the woman who taught me everything I know about the career world today. Also Tom (dad) for being such a loving father and poppy.

Finally I am most grateful to the grace of God who leads, guides and inspires my family and I every day. Psalm 32v8.

SOURCES

Page 17
'If you don't stand for something, you will fall for anything.'
Dr. Gordon Eadie
www.goodreads.com 25th June 2015

Page 18
'The best time to plant a tree was 20 years ago. The second best time is now.'
Chinese proverb
www.psychologytoday.com 25th June 2015

Page 91
'Passion is energy. Feel the power that comes from focusing on what excites you.'
Oprah Winfrey
www.goodreads.com 25th June 2015

Page 101
'Remember to treat others as they want to be treated in the interview—not how you wish to be treated.'
Alison Mooney
Pressing the Right Buttons

Page 166
'Your goals are your blueprints for the future. Goals are dreams about to be born. Goals are the ladders we climb to reach our vision of success. If you don't have goals, you end up working for someone who does have goals.'
John Eric Jacobsen
www.jacobsenprograms.com 25th June 2015

UK £14.99
US $19.99